THE
WITCH'S
SHIELD

PRAISE FOR CHRISTOPHER PENCZAK

The Witch's Shield

"This is a wise, helpful book for beginners and intermediate students of the craft."

—*Publishers Weekly*

"A treasure trove of traditional and new creative ways to protect yourself, your loved ones, and your property."

—*Dancing World Review*

The Witch's Coin

"Offers profound healing for the many among us who possess conflicted relationships with money and prosperity. I highly recommend this book."

—Judika Illes, author of
The Encyclopedia of 5000 Spells and *Pure Magic*

"Christopher Penczak provides a refreshing examination of the connection between money, magic, and the attitude people put toward both."

—Taylor Ellwood, editor of
Manifesting Prosperity: A Wealth Magic Anthology

THE
WITCH'S
SHIELD

PROTECTION MAGICK & PSYCHIC SELF-DEFENSE

CHRISTOPHER PENCZAK

Llewellyn Publications
Woodbury, Minnesota

First Edition
Eighteenth Printing, 2021

Book design by Donna Burch
Cover image © PhotoDisc
Cover design by Ellen Lawson
Edited by Andrea Neff
Interior illustrations by the Llewellyn art department

Library of Congress Cataloging-in-Publication Data

Penczak, Christopher.
    The witch's shield : protection magick & psychic self-defense / Christopher Penczak.
        p.   cm.
    Includes bibliographical references and index.
    ISBN 13: 978-0-7387-0542-2
    ISBN 10: 0-7387-0542-X
        1. Protection magick. 2. Self-defense—Psychic aspects. 3. Witchcraft. I. Title.

    BF1623.P75 2004
    133.4'3—dc22

                                                                            2004048334

Llewellyn Publications
A Division of Llewellyn Worldwide Ltd.
2143 Wooddale Drive
Woodbury, MN 55125-2989
www.llewellyn.com
Llewellyn is a registered trademark of Llewellyn Worldwide Ltd.

Printed in the United States of America

OTHER RELEASES BY
CHRISTOPHER PENCZAK

City Magick: Urban Spells, Rituals and Shamanism

Spirit Allies: Meet Your Team from the Other Side

The Inner Temple of Witchcraft:
Magick, Meditation and Psychic Development

The Inner Temple of Witchcraft CD Companion

Gay Witchcraft: Empowering the Tribe

The Outer Temple of Witchcraft: Circles, Spells and Rituals

The Outer Temple of Witchcraft CD Companion

Magick of Reiki

Sons of the Goddess: A Young Man's Guide to Wicca

The Temple of Shamanic Witchcraft:
Shadows, Spirits and the Healing Journey

The Temple of Shamanic Witchcraft CD Companion

The Mystic Foundation

Instant Magick: Ancient Wisdom, Modern Spellcraft

Ascension Magick: Ritual, Myth & Healing for the New Aeon

The Living Temple of Witchcraft Volume One: The Descent of the Goddess

The Living Temple of Witchcraft, Volume One CD Companion

The Living Temple of Witchcraft Volume Two: The Journey of the God

The Living Temple of Witchcraft, Volume Two CD Companion

The Temple of High Witchcraft: Ceremonies, Spheres and The
Witches' Qabalah

The Temple of High Witchcraft Meditation CD Companion

The Witch's Coin: Prosperity and Money Magick

The Witch's Shield: Protection Magick and Psychic Self-Defense

The Witch's Heart: The Magick of Perfect Love and Perfect Trust

ACKNOWLEDGMENTS

Thanks to Alixaendreia for her input and advice.

Thank you to Christian Medaglia and Claire Hart for their love and inspiration.

Thank you to all my teachers, and in particular Laurie Cabot and John Artimage from whose teachings I have drawn.

Special thanks to Colin Smith, Dorothy Morrison, Raven Grimassi, and Stephanie Taylor for their thought-provoking insights and for inspiring me to experience more, think more deeply, and express myself more clearly.

CONTENTS

Chapter 5

Becoming a Psychic Black Belt 81

Elemental Approach to Psychic Defense

Grounding

Grounding Techniques

Boundary

Protection Shield Techniques

Mental Flexibility

Direct Action

Spirit

Compassionate Defense

Chapter 6

Somebody's Watching Me 107

Evocation

Angels

Power Animals

Deities of Protection

Guardian Nature Spirits

Banishing Unwanted Spirits

Chapter 7

Banishings, Bindings, and Bottles 139

Casting a Magick Circle

The Right Time

Prevention Magick

Herbal Protection

Amulets

Wards

Guardian Beacon Spell

Direct Action Magick

Banishing Spells

Binding Spells

FIGURES

INTRODUCTION

The Witch's Shield is the first in a series of books designed to bring the magickal classroom directly to your home. I receive a lot of letters and e-mail from people who wish to attend my classes, or other magickal classes, but don't have access to them. They often want to take online classes or correspondence courses, which I don't currently offer. I like to teach in person, to directly guide students and lead them through the experiences of meditation and ritual. The biggest complaint about metaphysical books that I receive from people is the inability to do the meditations and exercises because they feel uncomfortable, lack confidence, and, in general, feel they lack the proper guidance to do them alone. Even those who have taken a class have difficulty re-creating the experience at home. For students with such problems, I have created this series of witchcraft books.

The Witch's Shield is based on one of my most popular classes in protection magick and psychic defense. Everyone seems to want protection, but very few people feel centered and protected in their personal

1

power. A controversial point about writing any protection magick book is that in order to teach readers how to understand and defend themselves from any type of attack, the author first has to explain the mechanism by which one can do an attack. But I strongly feel that imparting the knowledge of psychic protection outweighs the risk of revealing the methods of psychic attack. Like martial artists, one must understand the attack forms in order to become a competent defender.

Witches, pagans, and magicians take my protection magick and psychic defense course, but many people involved in other arts take it too, from aspiring shamans to dream workers. In *The Witch's Shield,* I outline and expand upon the basic steps of psychic defense, which the foundation materials found in other traditions and courses often lack.

As part of my "take home" class, this book contains the essence of my lecture and class discussion. Without a group, you can miss out on the discussion and sharing experiences that enrich a workshop, so I highly suggest that you reflect on each of the chapters. If you can, study the lessons with a friend or group of friends, so you can share your experiences.

In addition, the accompanying CD is a recording of the meditations and rituals to be done in class, so you can directly experience, with guidance, the lessons you have learned, and incorporate them into your everyday life. The exercises don't require extensive preparatory work or an in-depth knowledge of magickal theory, unlike my year-long course books found in the Temple of Witchcraft series. The lessons are simple and direct, to be used as needed.

I wish you much love, guidance, joy, and protection as you walk the path of the wise, the path of the witch, regardless of the path or tradition you follow. You don't have to give up your own path or identity to carry the witch's shield of Perfect Love and Perfect Trust into life with you.

Blessed Be,
Christopher Penczak

CHAPTER 1

WHO'S AFRAID OF THE BIG BAD WOLF?

Why do we need protection magick? Many magickal rituals, first and foremost the Witch's Circle, have strong elements of protection in their wording, even if the spell is for love, money, or healing. So invariably someone asks, "Why do we need protection? What's out there to get us? Is this magick dangerous?" Unfortunately, there are no easy answers to these questions.

Thoughts turn to the Hollywood horror films of demons, devils, and evil spirits. Such propaganda and stereotypes, which were perpetuated during the Dark and Middle Ages by the dominant religion and then brought to life through movie special effects, poison the magickal heart. They prevent us from feeling the magickal rhythms of life.

By our very nature, as embodiments of the divine, we seek a magickal life, but few of us ever find it or believe it is really possible, because of the exaggerated horrors perpetuated over the last two thousand years by religious leaders, reductionist science, and the media. This disconnection from the magick of life is one of the great problems facing the world today. Regardless of their personal spiritual path, most people don't feel connected to the patterns and cycles of life, and therefore can ignore the destruction we face as a species. Without the magickal life, as portrayed in the highest arts of witchcraft and paganism, humanity does not assume the role of caretaker, guardian, and partner with nature. Lack of this crucial identity has lead to the current spiritual crisis, and at the heart of this problem is our fear of the magickal.

We, as a society, call the magickal world the *occult*. The word occult has garnered sinister implications: "Be aware if your kids are involved in the occult. They are turning to evil forces!" I remember that when I was a teenager, my parents were told by a "good, God-fearing woman" that my interest in science fiction, fantasy, and role-playing games such as *Dungeons & Dragons* would turn me to the Devil because they were part of the occult. But these outlets were the only things that fed my magickal soul. Even though they are fiction and not true magick, such books, art, and music can sustain people who are seeking a magickal life, even if they don't know precisely what they are seeking. New Age books and stores were not readily available when I was a teenager, and even if they were, I was not in a place to appreciate them. I was brainwashed by society to believe that at best, such things are only fantasy and folklore that have no basis in real experiences, or at worst, that these games and books are tools of the Devil.

Witches and pagans believe that the Devil is a construct of the Christian church, gathered from many different mythologies and given a medieval spin-doctor treatment to use fear to force conversion and give the institution of the church a scapegoat when things did not go according to plan. The pagans were bullied into accepting

Christianity because they were told that their gods were evil spirits, and, in particular, that the horned gods of the land and animals were devils. The concept of ultimate good and ultimate evil has no place in paganism, as it has no place in nature. Life is too complex for such judgmental polarities. As a witch, I learned that one does not fear the God and Goddess, but loves and respects them, building a personal relationship with them through meditation, nature, and magick. We could never use the excuse that the Devil tempted us, since regardless of our motivations, we are wholly responsible for our actions and their consequences. We don't believe in a Devil who tempts us.

The word occult is not synonymous with the word evil; it means "hidden" or "obscured from view" and refers to information that is not generally known, found, or easy to understand. All the mystical arts are traditionally the province of those few who are interested in them. Most people are more worried about day-to-day survival and fulfillment, and have less interest in intensive introspection, meditation, and spirituality, which are the keys to a rewarding mystical practice in any tradition. The occult is the mystery of life that must be brought into view to be understood.

We call magick, psychic abilities, divination, and spirit work supernatural, but what does that mean? Super-nature is the natural world in its more heightened, magickal state. The word supernatural connotes something out of this world and unnatural. It is anything but. When one taps into the supernatural, one is tapping into the primal nature that runs through everything and everyone. That is divinity in action. There is nothing more natural than magick, for it is our human partnership with the natural forces. The root word of witch, *wicca,* is usually translated as "to bend or shape," which refers to the gentle bending, shaping, and partnering with the tides of life.

Fear of magick is really the fear of our own personal power and responsibility. It is usually easier to give such things away, to an institution, religion, or society, but such a lack of awareness leads to an imbalance. We have covered this imbalance with our many images of the bogeyman, the mysterious evil force, the Devil, or archetypal big bad wolf knocking at our door, threatening our lives. Even our fear-based images are ripe with our disconnection from the truth. Darkness is the symbol of life, the womb of the Goddess. The horned pagan gods are often protectors and fathers. The wolf is a powerful totem animal of protection. If we knew these magickal realities, our fears would dissolve away.

The truth of the matter is that magick, ritual, and spell work is no more dangerous than walking across the street. If you live in a busy city, that could be fairly dangerous, yet you still do it. The key is safety. All things in life carry some inherent risks. If anyone tells you otherwise, they are lying. You never know for certain where danger can come from, but you don't let that fear prevent you from living your life. When you cross the street, you look both ways. You watch the lights and stay alert. If you do this, then you most likely will have a safe experience crossing the street. If you don't, then you might have an accident.

Magick is the same way. The majority of the time, all is safe. If you are educated and careful, you will be fine. Protection and psychic defense are like having the tools you need in case things don't go according to your plan. Ideally, you will never need them, but like a good Boy Scout or Girl Scout, you are prepared. They are skills you will learn, possess, and grow with, and soon they will become second nature to your magickal way of life. You will live a protected magickal life always, wherever you go.

The horror stories I hear at times are from people with no education in magick who attempt complex spells they read about somewhere by jumping to the back of a book, rather than doing all the preliminary work to prepare for it. If they perform one spell that works well, they feel they are "advanced" or "gifted" and don't need to do any preliminary work. They may be gifted, but that's no way to learn an art, science, and spiritual path. You have to have all three aspects in balance along with any talent you have. It's like saying you successfully walked blindfolded across a busy street once, so you automatically assume that since you were safe that one time, you will always be safe. That's just asking for trouble.

IS PSYCHIC ATTACK REAL?

Yes, psychic attack is real. That's the easy answer. It is real because we experience it as real, and that is the bottom line to someone who is experiencing a psychic attack. Being in the profession of a public witch and teacher, I have gotten many calls from clients over the years who were certain that someone had cursed them. I noticed a pattern: so many people felt their "misfortune" was someone else's fault. They would not even consider the idea that perhaps their own thoughts and feelings were coming into play, that they were partners in the creation of their own misery. Nope. It was someone else's fault and it was my job to fix it for them.

I don't fix things for people. I help them transform and protect themselves. One of the ways I do this is by teaching techniques so you can be protected anytime. One of my favorite bits of wisdom is from the famous Chinese philosopher Lao-tzu: "Give a man a fish and you feed him for a day. Teach him how to fish and you feed him for a lifetime." I try to apply that to all my work.

When I first taught the workshop on which this book is based, I started by trying to break this blame-game/victim/fix-it mentality. I began by saying that 90 percent of all psychic attacks are not attacks, but rather self-created illusions. Though this is true, it doesn't help the person experiencing the attack. My tough love approach is not the best approach when one is experiencing a psychic attack and doesn't know what to do. We currently live in a society that is often fix-it/victim-oriented, and our natural reaction is to have someone take care of things when they go wrong. If you don't realize you are actively involved in any psychic attack experience you perceive, then how can you be expected to fix it yourself? It is only when you experience it for yourself that you can sympathize with others who experience it.

With that in mind, I have found that the majority of psychic attacks, curses, and hauntings were not what they appeared to be at first glance. Humans, as a whole, tend to jump to conclusions to support their own biases or fears. It takes awareness, introspection, and spiritual techniques to determine what is occurring and how best to resolve it. Through this work, we will practice these techniques together.

ATTRACTING ATTENTION

Why do those involved in magick, occultism, witchcraft, and healing seem to have more than their share of psychic attack experiences and a greater need for protection magick than "ordinary" people who seem to get along fine without it? A common assumption is that people involved in the magickal arts are a little wacky, paranoid, or delusional, but usually that is not the case.

Those of us involved in magickal practices have spent time expanding our awareness and sensitivity to subtle, unseen energies. Most people have little conscious perception of the subtle energies permeating us and our environments. I firmly believe that almost anyone can perceive the subtle, but we are simply not encouraged in mainstream society to develop these skills. Some people are naturally inclined to sense subtle energies, and seek training in traditions such as witchcraft to help them cope with this expanded awareness.

Witches, magicians, and shamans also attract more attention from the unseen forces. One teacher describes magickal ability as being like a flame. Most people radiate an average amount of light from their personal flame, blending into the psychic background with everybody else. They are not even consciously aware of their own light, or any other form of subtle energy. When you are aware of subtle energy and actively fan your own flame through magickal practices, then your flame grows brighter. Activities such as regular ritual, using Tarot cards, and daily meditation all expand our inner flame. This expansion of light attracts more attention, creating a beacon for those with the ability to see it, human and non-human. As you grow, for a while you attract more attention. Often it is benign, or neutral, but if you are perceptive, you feel a sense of presence. That sense of being watched can create an uneasy feeling.

Then, as you grow, your light balances out. As you find your own true will, your true purpose, your light fills its place within the pattern of the universe. Unless part of your purpose requires you to receive a lot of attention, your light fills in the spiritual background pattern and goes relatively unnoticed and untouched, only attracting the powers and people that will help you fulfill your purpose.

Certain New Age philosophies are structured around a fear-based polarity where the light is in a constant battle with the dark. They believe that the brighter your light shines, the more you will attract the forces of darkness and have to battle them. This is another rationale for the whole good-versus-evil, God-versus-Devil argument that has no real place in magickal work. I've had the honor of being among many people who are great spiritual lights, who go about their work with little drama or conflict. If you expect conflict, you will magickally create it and receive it. If you expect and create peace, you will receive peace.

Many practitioners in all traditions create conflict consciously or unconsciously as a way to feel more important in the grand scheme of things, but I've found that such individuals are not as important as those who create healing and peace from any conflict. As you claim more of your magickal power, reflect on what you wish to create.

PSYCHIC DANGERS

When you are in need of protection, the dangers are not always what they seem, but the need for protection is still very clear. A person not involved in real magick, whose only "knowledge" of magick comes from Hollywood movies, would assume that the only time we need protection is to banish evil spirits or defend ourselves from a "bad" witch, but our potential dangers come in many forms.

Though I am a huge proponent of ruling out all the most common forms of harm, most witches, myself included, are not Pollyannas about the existence of harmful spirits and people. Just because we don't believe in an ultimate source of evil, like the Christian Devil, does not mean that people's strong intentions and beliefs have not created thoughtforms and constructs of evil, or that less-than-loving spirits don't answer to the various names of the devil to receive attention and energy from humans. But before you consider such esoteric possibilities, look for a simpler answer. There is a wide spectrum of forms of danger that are much more mundane. Here are some possibilities:

Physical Harm

Protection magick is very useful for protecting oneself from any type of physical harm. Some people focus their defensive magick on purely psychic dangers and never cast spells for physical safety. Spells can be used to protect the body as well as the soul. Protection magick doesn't block fists or deflect speeding bullets, but works in a subtle way, intuitively guiding a person out of the path of potential harm. If it is working, you will never know how, beyond the fact that you are safe from harm.

Harmful Energy

"Harmful energy" is a phrase I use where other people say "negative energy." I don't use the term negative energy and strongly suggest that other people don't use it in ritual with me. Denoting "negative" with "bad" and "positive" with "good" is another polarizing New Age concept. Although the intention behind such words is clear, the literal meaning is not, since negative/positive refer to an electrical charge, and things like negative ions can be healthy for you. Anything that brings you out of balance is "bad," but it is not necessarily negative. If it is something that causes harm, disruption, or imbalance, then call it harmful, unbalanced, or discordant energy.

Harmful energy is not always conscious. Usually it is a very unconscious remnant from day-to-day living. Arguments, violence, grief, depression, stress, and illness can leave unbalanced energy in an environment that lingers, like dust balls under the bed. Most people don't know how to clean them up, because they can't "see" them, so they remain there for quite a while. We all go through tough times, but if the feelings seem to linger, then perhaps it is the energy of the time that remains, even if the situation has resolved itself.

Harmful energy can be found anywhere and can create situations that cause physical, mental, and emotional discomfort, from headaches and nausea to feeling trapped in emotional/mental patterns. Usually it is not a big deal to most people, because they are so used to it. It's like living in a dirty house. Harmful energy is a problem for psychically sensitive people who lack control over their psychic abilities, leaving them open to the energy. It can also be a problem for magickal practitioners if not cleared up before doing ritual, spells, or psychic work.

Harmful Judgments

All thought is energy, and when someone directs a thought toward you, they are directing an energy. When someone thinks something, even without saying it, they can affect your energy, mood, and strength if you are not centered in your own power and sense of self.

In class, I do exercises with groups to prove this, since most people don't believe it. I have one person come up to the front of the room, and we test that person's strength through traditional kinesiology, also known as muscle-testing, a technique used in many holistic services. Muscle testing can be used to find out if a particular substance enhances or weakens an individual.

First, we determine the person's baseline strength level, which we can then use to gauge if a new substance strengthens or weakens the person. The person holds out his dominant arm at a right angle from the body, and attempts to hold it in place as I place pressure on it, trying to force it down. From this simple test, I can get an idea of the person's normal strength.

Next, I have the person hold a substance in his nondominant hand, usually pressing it up to his chest and letting its energy interface with his own personal energy. The substance can be anything from a crystal to an herb or vitamin supplement. I repeat the test by pressing down on the dominant arm and determining whether the substance increases or decreases the person's strength. If it increases his strength, then I would have him carry the crystal or take the supplement. If the test weakens his arm, then the substance is not good for him.

Next, I have the rest of the group send strong thoughts to the person, cuing them silently through cards as to whether the thoughts should be complimentary or derogatory. When people think things like "I love you," "You are beautiful," or "You are strong," the person, without even physically hearing these words, is strengthened. When the group thinks things like "I hate you," "You are ugly," "You are weak," or any put-down, the person's strength level grows weak. This change occurs without the person actually hearing a word.

So when someone judges you in a nonconstructive way, they may be sending harmful energy to you. This doesn't mean we should not judge or compare things in our daily life, but the spirit in which we do so plays a critical role. You can judge someone's work as faulty, or dislike something about the person, but when you judge the entire person to be faulty or no good, you are potentially harming them. Name calling is a form of psychic attack. Hatred, jealousy, and anger are also forms of psychic attack, even though they are often unintentional. We are not trained to realize that our words and thoughts have power.

Harmful Projections

Projections are like spells. Projection is the act, conscious or unconscious, of sending our energy into the future to manifest. Witches and mages choose to project consciously, through ritual and meditation, even if it is for something as simple as getting a parking space near the door.

Most people, however, project thoughts unconsciously, and in a detrimental way to themselves and others. As an extension of harmful judgments, harmful projections are like judgments of the future. If you think to yourself that someone will never be successful, never be healthy, never find true love, or never amount to anything, you are sending out a harmful projection. Most people don't mean to do this—its an unconscious aspect of our culture—but now we must become conscious. Again, the spirit in which the thought or word is projected is the most important thing. You can have discernment and explore possibilities without condemning another.

The Evil Eye

No book on protection magick would be complete without a talk about the evil eye. My maternal grandmother was involved in folk magick and talked about how to cure the evil eye. I always thought it strange, since no one had really explained what it was. The evil eye was often blamed for anything that went bad by the older generations of my family. When you are raised in a culture, like many first- and second-generation Italian Americans, that understands and accepts such realities, then belief in the evil eye is more prevalent. Looking back on it, I started to think it was a part of the blame-game/victim mentality I wanted my own family, students, and clients to break, but there is a sound metaphysical underpinning to the evil eye.

From a shamanic or energetic point of view, the evil eye—which is, literally, directing harmful energy from your eyes to another's—sends a disruptive force into the spiritual bodies or chakra column of the victim, disrupting the line of connection between the personal self and the higher self and guides. If you are on the receiving end of the evil eye, your sense of protection and guidance from your spiritual allies is disrupted. Your intuitive awareness from these allies is temporarily dulled or blocked. You are not guided on your path, out of harm's way, which makes you vulnerable to sickness, accidents, and a sense of misfortune from being in the wrong place at the wrong time. Most practitioners of the evil eye don't have such a sophisticated understanding of the mechanics involved. They simply do it because they know it works.

The evil eye is much like harmful judgments and projections, but it is a conscious and knowing projection of harm. It is when someone with a little knowledge and understanding knowingly wishes harm or bad luck upon a person or family, usually because they have an axe to grind. You could call this a "curse," but I reserve that word for another category. If the evil eye is a curse, then it is usually a folk magick curse, or an amateur curse, regardless of the sender's delusions of power and grandeur. More often than not, at least in modern Western culture, it is usually devoid of a belief in magick; the giver of the evil eye is cursing in fantasy, having no real solid belief that thoughts are energy and can affect another. But they still can.

Time Traps

Time traps are an extension of the evil eye by someone with a little more knowledge. Rather than projecting a vague wish for harm or bad luck, the user of a time trap has a specific harmful event they wish to create for someone, and sends that thought out through words or visualization. Usually, the victim's misfortune creates some sense of good fortune or well-being for the perpetrator. Again, like the evil eye, most people don't believe in the power of thought and intent, and such time traps are relegated to the realm of fantasy or malicious wishful thinking; but when you fantasize about the misfortune of others, you are still sending out psychic harm.

Psychic Vampires

A popular term in the New Age and occult worlds, a *psychic vampire* is one who drains others of their energy, vitality, and emotion. I hate the term, but feel compelled to use it so there is no misunderstanding. The phrase psychic vampire is used synonymously with *energy vampire* and *spiritual vampire*. The word vampire conjures up a dark, gothic image of one purposely going out and doing harm, a creature of evil. Most people who are categorized as psychic or energy vampires are not conscious of what they are doing, and don't understand the mechanics involved, usually because they are raised in a world that doesn't understand or accept psychic energy. Most of these people are not in a place of spiritual health or power, and are often plagued with physical, mental, or emotional issues and depression.

When such "vampires" find a person who is bright and vital, they seek to be with that person, subconsciously hoping to draw from that experience and be more like the vital person. But instead of raising their own energy and vibration, changing their patterns to match the higher vibration of light and enthusiasm, they end up bringing the other person down. They psychically feed on the energies of vital people to fill the holes in their own energy bodies.

Most often, the psychically healthy people don't understand the energy dynamic and can't prevent the drain. All they know is that when a certain "vampire" comes around, the one with the perpetual black cloud hanging overhead, they feel drained. Instead of trying to create a situation of healing and support, they withdraw from the situation.

The "vampires" simply want to feel better, but then feel worse as people start to shun them, spiraling further into depression and darkness. The important thing to realize is that we all go through such periods when we are clingy and needy and don't know how to handle it. When we understand the energy dynamics, we can seek support from others without being a drain, and we can support others without being drained ourselves.

Only in rare circumstances do certain psychic vampires understand the mechanics of what they are doing and take a pleasure in being able to drain power from others. They can rationalize and justify their actions, but it is a process of creating inappropriate boundaries, justifying the use of protection magick. These actions can create an unhealthy energetic pattern that is a basis for harmful magick.

Unenlightened Gurus

I use the term *unenlightened guru* as a friendly code name for potential cult leaders. In the spiritual worlds, mainstream and New Age, certain personalities can become the focus of great psychic energy from their followers. Some are caught unawares and don't know what to do with this authority, and flounder. Some try to be as empowering as possible to their disciples. Sadly, many relish the opportunity and power, and knowingly or unknowingly begin using the psychic energy of others for their own personal gain, pleasure, or amusement, acting as powerful psychic vampires. Most are not bad people. Like the psychic vampire, they do this unknowingly and are overwhelmed by the new sensations. There are others, however, who are psychically savvy enough to know exactly what they are doing, and enjoy their powerful role very much, building a cult of personality around themselves and their newfound sense of power.

Unwanted Spirits

When it comes to the need for protection magick, most people are not as worried about people in the physical world as they are about entities in the spirit world. Just as the physical world is populated with myriad beings, so are the spirit worlds. Most of the beings who are initially drawn to us are helpful spirit guides, waiting for us to notice them.

The other most common spiritual encounter is the equivalent of scavengers on the astral plane. When you stoke your magickal flame, all manner of critters check you out. Some of them are mischievous or playful. Like rodents, insects, or reptiles, they are not everyone's favorite experience, but they are a part of creation. They are relatively harmless, and go away once they realize you are harmless to them as well. Donald Michael Kraig, author of the classic *Modern Magick*, calls them the "little nasties," and I love that name. The protection techniques in this book are enough to always banish these spirits. Just like our animal scavengers, I respect their right to life, but don't necessarily want the equivalent of a rat crawling on me when I meditate.

The second type of unwanted spirit usually comes in the form of the earthbound dead. These are the ghosts of folklore, the energy of those who have passed on from this world, but have not yet crossed over into the next. An unfinished task, act of violence, shock, or great injustice usually prevents them from finding their way to the next realm. Some ghosts are fully conscious souls, while most are echoes and fragments of who they once were, astral shells attached to the world and left behind in the lowest vibrations of the ethers.

The third type of unwanted spirit is called a larvae in some traditions. Larvae are considered to be vampiric thoughtforms, and have mixed and mingled with our lore on vampires. These thoughtforms, constructs of mental energy, are usually created by humans, intentionally or unintentionally. They can start out as obsessions or even mystical practices and spells, but are forgotten. To maintain their existence, they need more energy, and will attach to a person or place, slowly draining vital life force. They are usually quite unconscious, since they are not truly complete, conscious spirits and are simply doing what is needed to survive. Larvae are not necessarily malevolent or frightening, though they can be. Ultimately, they are bad for our health, like a parasite living off our blood, and must be removed.

The last type of unwanted spirit is a malevolent spirit. They can be the spirits of the dead not at rest, but more typically they are spirits who were not necessarily human to begin with. They are spirits bound by anger, fear, and other shadow emotions. Some are thought-forms created by magicians throughout the ages but never banished. Others are pockets of harmful energy and thought created by the general populace, eventually taking on a persona. When unaware magicians and witches summon spirits from the other world, but do not banish or release them, the spirits can remain bound and unhappy in this world. They are more likely to manifest in frightening and violent forms.

Elemental beings, those summoned and never banished properly, or those nature spirits simply living out of balance due to the environmentally unaware actions of humanity, can be in a state of unrest and project feelings of malevolence that sensitive humans feel. The spirits in some sites in nature are quite loving and welcoming. But when hiking, say, in other areas, you can feel a sense of dread from spirits who do not want to be disturbed, who actively ward away humanity, usually to protect a site.

Some New Age traditions with a polarized view of light and dark feel that there is a hierarchy of spirits that come from love and light. Likewise, there must be a hierarchy of spirits, entities, masters, and magicians who don't come from love, and who seek to cause harm, strife, discord, temptation, and a host of emotions that would be labeled negative, such as anger, hate, fear, lust, greed, and jealousy. This is the primary concept of angelic and demonic conflicts.

Although the concept of angels and demons can be found in ancient cultures, the current polarized view of them does not fit into the modern Wiccan viewpoint. Our ancient ancestors in the witchcraft traditions did not see things in such absolute extremes. All things contain spectrums, not absolutes, including spirits. Historically, you don't see the polarized division of good and evil until the Zoroastrian religion, and its influence in the Judeo-Christian-Islam faiths. If you examine the medieval codices of demon names used by Judeo-Christian magicians, you will find that many of their names and symbols are corruptions of the ancient pagan gods.

Curses

I define a curse as "a specific harmful spell done by another magickal practitioner." This person has full knowledge of the working of spells and is purposely using that knowledge to cause harm. I used to think that this form of harm was rare, because one of the main tenets of most magickal traditions is that energy returns to its source—what you do comes back to you threefold, whether helpful or harmful. In witchcraft, we call this the Law of Three, or the Law of Return. This threefold rule encourages those with magickal knowledge and ability to aid others. Our only ethic is the Wiccan Rede: "And it harm none, do what you will." This includes yourself.

I thought that such realities would inhibit those who have direct knowledge of magick from ever doing such work, but I'm disappointed to say that with the growing interest in magick and the availability of such material, quite a few unhealthy magickal practitioners are using the arts for harm. There have always been those who misuse magick. I wish it weren't true, but I have to take my head out of the sand. Such unpleasant truths are one reason why books like this are needed.

Those with higher levels of knowledge can create or summon powerful spirits and send them to plague their rivals. But if you are protected and centered in your power, you will deflect such entities. Even if the spirits are not deflected, it is their nature to return to their sender and plague the sender, who cannot easily repel or banish them at that stage.

Psychic Attack

Psychic attack is much like a curse, but is done by one who is not necessarily using the tools of ritual magick. The effect can be the same. Practitioners of psychic attack use no altar, candles, symbols, or other tools, but simply focus their will with the intent of causing harm, pain, or misfortune upon a specific person. Again, just as in magick, what you send out returns to you, but this cold, hard fact does not discourage those involved from launching these base attacks. Somehow, people who believe psychic attack is a valid option feel they are above the laws of return in the universe, that they are somehow exempt. They feel they are cosmic arbiters of justice; if they are miserable, then they have a right to cause others misery, without experiencing any repercussions. Ultimately, this only causes more misery for them in the long run.

Mesmerism

Though many would consider mesmerism a form of psychic attack, the result is not spiritual or physical damage, but a suppression of will. Some people are so charming and convincing that they have a psychic hypnotic effect on others that suppresses their individual will in favor of what the mesmerist wants. In effect, mesmerism is much like a form of mind control or, in extreme cases, brainwashing.

Like psychic vampirism, most mesmerists do it unintentionally or, at the very least, don't believe there is anything magickal or psychic about it. They simply feel they are persuasive or good talkers and make a convincing case. There is nothing dramatically harmful in the long run because the mesmerist is not consciously using his full will or putting a harmful intent into the situation. But when the discernment and intuition of the person being targeted is dramatically suspended, something else is going on.

Again, like psychic vampirism, some realize what they are doing, realize the power involved, and consciously use it to their advantage, even getting "high" off the sense of power. Cult leaders are often accused of practicing this type of mesmerism, which results in fanatical behavior and loyalty in their followers. Some metaphysicians explain the psychic mechanics involved as the mesmerist projecting vital life force, known as prana or akasha, out of his or her eyes, programmed with the intention to charm, seduce, and control. Unlike the evil eye, the energy of mesmerism is not direct and jarring, but soft and seductive, used to enrapture the target.

Prayer

Prayer can be wonderful, but like anything else, in the wrong hands it can be a tool of harm, falling somewhere between curses and psychic attack, but deserving its own category. Those who "pray" for witches, magicians, gays, lesbians, and liberals can be doing harmful magick. Ideally, I would hope they are praying for love and for the highest divine good, but many pray with the hope that others will see things "their"way, because they believe it is the only true way. They pray for others to give up their "sinful" beliefs and actions. This is a form of psychic attack, just as unethical as any other, and you will find it not only in the conservative right-wing culture, but also among certain holier-than-thou New Agers.

Ancestral Energies

Energies can be passed on from one family member to another, like inheriting particular physical traits such as hair or eye color, or an aptitude for music, art, or sports. Such energies include blessings, gifts, and helpful spirits, but can also take the form of what are considered family curses. They are like family karma. Some are actually harmful energies passed from one family member to another at birth. Others are unresolved issues and conflicts generated by the ancestor, such as feelings of intense fear, regret, loneliness, or anger. Energy cannot be destroyed, but can simply be transformed. If one does not transform a certain unwanted energy before death, and it was the wish of the sender to curse the family as well, then the energy can be passed on to future generations.

Unresolved emotions, such as not living for yourself, can be passed on to others. Sometimes such energies dissipate over time and generations, but some are strongly persistent and need to be consciously broken through life choices that lead to spiritual cleansing and release. If your family "curse" is the belief that you can never be happy in your job, created by generations of ancestors unhappy in their jobs, consciously choosing a satisfying career, no matter what, will break that cycle for you.

Past-Life Energies

Some people believe that unwanted harmful energies can attach themselves to us at a soul level, and transition with us from life to life until we resolve the issue. They may be apparent from birth, or become activated when we come into a similar situation in this life. If we were cursed in a past life, there is a possibility the we will carry that curse, or past patterns of it, in this lifetime. Sometimes it is difficult to distinguish between the consequences of past-life actions (our karma) and past-life curses, but meditation, introspection, and honest awareness will help you resolve it either way.

Yourself

Sometimes you are the greatest source of harm to your own magickal well-being. Your own lack of awareness, low self-esteem, critical self-judgments, distorted boundaries, unresolved emotions, and personal fears can contribute to simulating any of the psychic-attack scenarios just described. People filled with fear see evil spirits all around them. People filled with anger see people who are angry and out to get them. The world is your mirror, and you can be your own worst enemy and self-saboteur. So before you go looking for another to blame, look in the mirror and realize that on some level, for some reason, you are involved in the process, so take responsibility for your end of it.

OUT OF BOUNDS

The core issue of any situation where we are in need of protection is boundary. Whenever we are violated, physically, mentally, emotionally, or psychically, our sense of boundaries has been violated. When we harm another, we have crossed a boundary. All sources of psychic harm essentially boil down to boundary issues. We knowingly or unknowingly cross a boundary, or allow our boundary to be crossed, without knowing how to stop it. The concepts of boundaries, territory, and space are found in all aspects of life, but creating a healthy model of them in real life is not that easy to do. Boundary symbols, from the magick circle to a protective shield, are repeated over and over again in both traditional magick and modern psychology.

In magick, we cast boundaries in ritual, creating a sacred space where energy is contained. We block out unwanted forces and spirits. We are protected from them in the sacred space. They cannot interfere with our work, as we invite in helpful spirits. Ritual creates a boundary between the day-to-day life and the mystical, with a boundary that opens the way, and one that signals the closing of the way.

Psychic defense works with the aura, our energetic boundary and personal space. When someone is psychically healthy, that person has a strong sense of personal space, but is adaptable to a given situation. The boundary is defined, but not rigid.

In psychology, our boundary is about containing and dealing with our own thoughts and feelings without projecting them onto others. Simultaneously, another boundary issue is to not accept the judgments or responsibilities of others as a part of our own identity.

My good friend and covenmate Jessica spent time in Wales as part of a semi-magickal, ecological farming community. Learning boundary issues was a great challenge for the group. One of their mantras was: "That's not my stuff. That's your stuff, and you need to deal with it." How rarely one person says that openly. In most of my experiences, we danced around the topic and hinted at it, but never said it openly. In Jessica's community, the phrase may have been

Figure 1: Pentacle

overused and embellished, but her tale and its setting showed me that boundaries of psychology, magick, and psychic health are all intertwined much more closely than we all think. The word psyche originally meant "soul," although we use it as a prefix to denote the mental as opposed to the physical, in the medical world. I hope we reclaim the full richness of the word, so we don't divide the soul from the mind, heart, body, and magick.

BALANCED PROTECTION

Whenever we approach an issue in need of shielding, protection or self-defense, I think we are well served to keep a balanced view of the situation. This prevents us from flying off the handle into reaction, drama, or conflict. Balance allows us to assess the situation and handle it from a stable place.

I use the model of the pentacle, with five elements, as my sign for balance and my greatest teacher (figure 1). In protection magick, the five elements stand for the following:

Earth: Grounding

Be practical and down-to-earth before anything else. Look for the simple, rational, everyday explanations before jumping to conclusions about psychic attack.

Water: Compassion

If you determine that someone or something is at the root of your issue, have compassion and sympathy for this person or entity. We only hurt others when we are feeling hurt. Remember a time when you have been hurt and you have caused hurt or have been tempted to hurt another. This does not excuse anyone's actions, but gives you the spiritual empathy needed to handle the situation with grace and compassion rather than anger.

Air: Understanding

Understanding refers to true knowledge of defense. Understand the mechanics of subtle energy, thought, will, and emotions. Understand the dynamics of self-defense. If you understand and live in your own truth and understand how to use your gifts, your true self cannot be harmed by another, regardless of their perceived power or ability.

Fire: Power

The only way to truly be protected at all times is to claim your personal power with the highest code of ethics and responsibility. If you are centered in this type of power, the power of the universe supports you, and no one and nothing can defeat you.

Spirit: Purpose

Understand that all events have a purpose in the greater pattern of the universe. Some fulfill their purpose in the highest, most conscious expression possible, while other people do not, yet they still fulfill a purpose on some level and serve the greater whole. Most often, the person who seems to be the least spiritually "evolved" will be the greatest teacher, serving the highest good by creating such magickal dramas to challenge our mastery of our own grounding, compassion, understanding, and power. Without such challenging experiences, we would not know how well we embody the four previous ideals of grounding, compassion, understanding, and power.

If you keep the principles of the pentacle in mind whenever you are challenged, you will handle the situation and maintain your boundaries with the greatest love, trust, and grace possible.

CHAPTER 2

IS THERE A WITCH DOCTOR IN THE HOUSE?

So now that you are aware of the potential psychic dangers, how do you definitively know that you are in need of protection? If you want to step out of the victim role, it can be a hard call. Either we tend to assume that someone else is always to blame, or we take the opposite approach and find fault at our own doorstep and no one else's. It's true that we all have a role to play in any dangerous situation, perceived or otherwise, because we attract such experiences based on our previous thoughts and actions. However, we have to find a middle ground where we take responsibility for our actions, but at the same time don't take on the responsibilities of others.

In the end, the basics of protection magick and psychic defense can be done at any time. Grounding yourself in your own sense of power and sacredness will never harm you. Even if you think you are overreacting to a situation, doing the banishing and clearing rituals in this book will cause no harm, and may even help you sort out the experience and gain a clearer perspective.

SYMPTOMS OF PSYCHIC OR MAGICKAL HARM

Potential symptoms of psychic or magickal harm from another, intentional or otherwise, include the following:

- A feeling that you are being watched by something creepy, unfriendly, or malevolent, particularly during a time of quiet reflection alone or when doing any spiritual work.

- A sense of heaviness or pressure, as if something were sitting on your chest or shoulders. This physical presence may be accompanied by a sense of cold or heat manifesting as a sudden change in an otherwise normal temperature, without a proper weather change in the environment to support such a temperature shift.

- Hearing voices of a malevolent nature. Usually these are "psychic voices" heard in the mind, but at times they can feel so real that they seem audible. Sometimes more than one person in the same vicinity can hear them at the same time.

- Unusual psychic manifestations of fearsome things. These manifestations can occur as obsessive thoughts of accidents or attacks, when you are not normally prone to obsessive thinking. Manifestations can also include visions. Some visions occur as brief but disturbing glimpses in day-to-day waking life. Others appear in full detail during meditations and rituals, interrupting your spiritual work.

- Vivid, recurring nightmares. Often, the images are of things that are generally considered fearsome, but are not necessarily your personal fears and phobias.

- A sharp, stabbing pain in the body. Such pain usually manifests as a headache. Traditionally, it is said to occur when the antagonist's name is mentioned in the presence of the target for psychic attack, or when the target thinks about the antagonist. This is often felt as a strong headache at the third eye without explanation, or as a sharp pain where the skull and neck meet. Pains could also be located at chakra points.

- A slow and steady drain on your personal energy. Such drains can affect your work and personal life, as well as your established magickal abilities and talents. Your intuition and ability to use energy and magick can diminish. This is usually accompanied by intense feelings of cold when you are not normally prone to being cold.

- An experience of psychic loss or entrapment. In certain traditions, harmful practitioners curse you by trapping a portion of your energy body and preventing it from returning to your body. Some consider this portion to be a part of your soul. You do not lose your soul itself, but what is considered a fragment or shard of your soul, in the shamanic traditions.

  Traumatic experiences can cause parts of our energy to fragment. If we do not heal and rest to integrate them, the trauma can cause them to leave our proximity and hide in the other worlds for safety. Healing, either of a shamanic or traditional nature, can usually coax these parts back to us, unless they are purposely blocked by another.

  In the Voodoo traditions, harmful practitioners are said to grab your *ti bon ange,* or "little angel," also referred to as the *astral body,* which travels when you sleep. They use spells to trap this little self in hope of exerting influence over the person in the waking world. Symptoms of this experience include a feeling of loss; a loss of power, purpose, or self-identity; a lack of will; a lack of interest in life or a walking-zombie-like attitude;

or going through the motions of life, but never fully participating. Other healers call this *ghost walking,* and it can occur either through harmful magick or naturally through trauma or illness.

• Losing many personal objects of importance when you are not naturally prone to misplace things.

• Suddenly becoming accident-prone when you are normally graceful. Accidents may cause you to break precious objects or to injure yourself or others, from bumps and bruises to more severe injuries.

• A sudden and unexpected illness when no other causes of the illness are apparent. If you are a witch or mystic in touch with your body, do a deep meditation and scan to determine the source of the illness and the message your body is giving you. If you can't find a cause, this can be a potential symptom of psychic attack.

In many folk magick traditions, practitioners of harmful magick would curse an entire family. Usually the weakest member of the family, the baby, is most susceptible to the harmful energy of the curse, and will experience an extended bout of colic that is not cured by traditional methods. In many indigenous traditions of healing, it is believed that many illnesses are caused by a source of harmful energy outside of the afflicted. If someone wishes you ill will, even unconsciously, it can manifest as illness or injury. Breaking the energy of ill will, or banishing the spirit of sickness, heals the illness.

• A long chain of events that can only be categorized as "bad luck," particularly in financial, personal, or romantic areas of life. Again, as when we look at illness as a potential symptom of psychic attack, you must be introspective to find the root of your "bad luck." Often we create the circumstances of our situation, and cannot blame them on other people wishing us ill. Just as illness can be a sign from our body and spirit telling us to find balance and healing, experiences with unfortunate circumstances can guide us to a life in greater harmony.

- An unconscious change in your physical upkeep and appearance, as if part of you were trying to hide. The few times that I felt I was the target of harmful psychic energy, I found myself not shaving for long periods of time, and constantly changing my facial hair and usual wardrobe, like I wanted to throw someone off my trail. I didn't realize I was doing this at the time. It was only in retrospect that I could see the reasons for my behavior.

- Any of the previous symptoms manifesting after receiving a strange, unexpected, or unwanted gift from either a stranger or from someone who you suspect means you harm. Practitioners of harmful magick will often link their curses and spells to objects, and transfer their harm through the object.

  A friend of mine received an expensive sweater from a very sickly woman who wanted my friend's job at a metaphysical store. As soon as she wore it, she became deathly ill. It was only after the sweater was buried with a protection ritual that her sickness left, as mysteriously as it began. I received a necklace under similar circumstances, but burned it before I ever wore it, recognizing its intent. My gift giver was surprised to see me up and around.

- An experience of partial or full possession. Possession is when a malevolent spirit, often referred to as a demon or devil, attempts to control a physical body. Partial possession creates the feeling that something foreign is attempting to take you over, or that you are simply not "alone" inside your body. Full possession ranges from the feeling that you have lost motor control of your body or that someone else has motor control of you, to the classic stereotypical images of possession with speaking in malevolent voices and foreign languages, physical contortions, and feats of strength. It is important to note that true, full possession is the least frequent occurrence of those listed, and that most recorded cases of demonic possession during the witch trials of Europe were most likely cases of ergot poisoning, a fungus growing on grain that produces a bad LSD-like effect and also confers temporary strength and madness.

Just because you have one or more of these symptoms does not guarantee that you are under magickal attack. As previously mentioned, sometimes you are your own worst enemy and need to reflect on that possibility.

When you break harmful energetic links using the techniques described in the subsequent chapters, you should experience a fairly immediate sense of relief from these symptoms.

The symptoms of psychic attack can manifest very quickly, and leave just as quickly. Recently, I was unintentionally taking on the psychic energy of a friend who was very upset with me. He is a powerful, yet often unfocused, witch. He did not intentionally wish me harm, but was very mad at me. I felt physically ill, with nausea, diarrhea, and a headache. The symptoms came on suddenly, and after suffering for a few hours, I intuitively felt that the source of illness was not me. Skipping the traditional diagnoses and questions, I simply did the Lesser Banishing Ritual of the Pentagram (see chapter 7) and found myself clear and pain-free. I then meditated on it, and felt my friend was the source of the illness. We talked on the phone and cleared up the misunderstanding. Even unintentional psychic attacks can do you harm, but the techniques of disengagement will bring swift relief and help you resolve the situation completely.

DENIAL

When being psychically attacked, two common reactions are to assume all responsibility or to assume none of the responsibility, but there is a third choice: denial. Not wanting to assume the blame, or cast blame anywhere else, and wanting to believe the best of all things in the universe, you turn a blind eye and pretend that everything is okay. Humans use denial all the time, in a variety of situations. It's easy to do when it comes to magickal things, because so much of the world doesn't believe in magick anyway. It's easy to go along with the crowd, even when we have had experiences that prove otherwise.

Denial is found in so much of our spiritual lore. It's easy to get trapped in it without even realizing it, or think we are being spiritual when, in fact, we are being foolish by not protecting ourselves.

We are told that all things are Divine, and divinity is love, so all things are love. Spirits and energies can't be bad, because they are love. What the sages meant by this is that all things are an expression of the divine, that there are many possibilities as to how that divinity can be expressed in the physical world. We must be aware of expressions of the divine that are inappropriate for us at the time, such as harmful people and situations, and draw the appropriate boundaries in our lives.

Much of our psychic lore says that if we focus on the "negative," we give it power, making it stronger and fueling conflict. Instead, we must be peaceful and centered. There is a difference between not actively engaging in a conflict and not acknowledging it as the current reality. When I look back at peaceful warriors, such as Gandhi, I see that they did not actively engage in violence, thereby continuing the cycle of violence, but they were certainly aware of the situation and consciously chose how to handle it. If you don't acknowledge a harmful situation, you cannot choose the highest path to deal with it. Without awareness of the situation, you cannot be sure you are not feeding it energy. Sometimes ignoring a bad situation gives it the time and space to grow stronger or more out of balance. Being unaware is not a trait of a healthy, competent witch.

I am often guilty of denying my fears, or simply trying to intellectualize them. Fear can be a teacher, just like any other dark emotion. In witchcraft, you must develop both your intuition and your intellect to be able to discern which fears must be overcome and which fears must be honored because they are teaching you to avoid someone or something harmful. Some fears have your best interests at heart. Pagan traditions teach us not to deny our fears, but to face them, as they are often embodied in the lessons of the underworld goddesses and gods. Images of the horned god and crone goddess are fearsome, but also come with love. I often look to people and situations I fear as aspects of the dark gods, and not something to demonize. I seek to embrace them and see the good, but at times, you have to protect yourself and create a boundary, and not embrace them.

Such fears must be honored, acknowledged, and listened to, instead of being dismissed or slowly contemplated. The true test of spiritual mastery is not to deny the message, but to hear it, act upon it, and still not be ruled by fear. Honoring fear is different from being consumed and overridden by it.

Another trap I fall into is automatically assuming my motivations are the same as everyone else's, that we have the same point of view. That's simply not true. If I can't imagine myself using magick to harm another, I have a hard time imagining another person, particularly other witches, using magick to harm another. How could they? Easy. Those witches do not subscribe to the same code of ethics and definitions of the word witch as I do. Although it's good to empathize with others, you can't blind yourself to the truth in an effort to see the good in all people.

PARANOIA

The flip side of denial is paranoia. While some people have a tendency to never acknowledge any harm directed toward them, others are just too willing to see a spiteful enemy behind every tree. Their worldview can range from one witch casting curses, to an entire coven, or even a global conspiracy. I love the old saying "Just because you are paranoid, doesn't mean they aren't out to get you." You must recognize that there can be harmful energy directed toward you, but pure paranoia shifts the focus to blame, rather than understanding why the situation was created and how you can both cure it and prevent if from happening again.

Those in a paranoid or victim mode often banish harm from one "source" and attract it from another, since the root of the imbalance, or the reason why they were open to such an experience, was never resolved. Through the forest path there may be denial on one side and paranoia on the other, but a witch strives to live in balance, seeing reality, even the magickal reality, as it is and not through the lens of unconsciousness or fear.

DIAGNOSIS

If you want to know for certain if someone or something is meaning you harm, but have no clear sense of it, you are on the right track. It is quite normal to doubt these things. If you are completely adamant one way or the other, I think that would be unhealthy. If the grounding and centering exercises of chapters 3, 5, and 6 don't bring you clarity, then I would try these other forms of divination. More importantly, if possible, I would seek out an unbiased opinion from a magickal practitioner who can do such divinations for you. Such people will not have an emotional attachment or energetic charge related to the situation and will have a clearer, unattached view.

You can choose from many different forms of divination. Ideally, if you are doing it for yourself, choose a method with which you have some familiarity and comfort. If you are seeking help from someone else, let them choose their most effective method for divining such matters.

Pendulum

When in doubt, use the pendulum. A pendulum is a weight tied to a cord. It can be fancy, with quartz-crystal points on a silver chain, or just a washer on a string. Many people use their necklace as a pendulum.

Before you use it, cleanse the tool (see chapter 3). Then sit meditatively and ask to connect to your higher guidance. Hold the pendulum still, and if it is the first time you have used it, your first question should be "What is a yes response?" Wait to see what the pendulum does. When you begin, the motion of the pendulum will be hard to perceive, but after a few moments, the swing of the pendulum will become clear. Then ask, "What is a no response?" Traditionally, yes is clockwise and no is counterclockwise, but always ask these questions for every new pendulum you try, because each pendulum and each person is different.

Then begin to ask yes or no questions to determine the source of your problem, such as: "Am I in need of protection at this time?" "Is someone causing me harm?" "Is it a physical, living person or a spirit?" "Is it conscious?" "Is it unintentional?" "Is it (name of person/spirit)?"

The pendulum can give definitive yes/no answers from your higher guidance when used in this manner, although many people feel they influence the pendulum to do what they want. It is very easy to make the pendulum turn the way you desire, even if you are not holding it and subconsciously moving it. Influencing the pendulum's movement is much like influencing the subject of a muscle test, as described in chapter 1. Certain thoughts directed toward the subject changed the response from a yes to a no, weakening the muscles. Strong thoughts can also change the answers from a pendulum, either giving you the answer you desire or the answer you fear. To get around this problem, I suggest visualizing a peaceful place with your eyes closed after you ask the question, with no attachment to the answer. After a few moments, open your eyes and see what the pendulum is telling you.

Tarot/Runes

Two of my favorite forms of divination are Tarot cards and Norse runes, although they leave much to be desired in terms of providing definitive yes/no answers. They do produce results that allow you to contemplate the situation on a deeper level. Getting definitive answers to your questions via these two divinatory methods can be hard to do for yourself, but if you must, I recommend that you first sit and meditate with the oracle. When ready, ask one general question about the situation, such as "Am I in need of magickal protection at this time?" or "Am I in danger at this time?" Then pull out one card or rune. If it is a "brighter" card or rune, I assume that I am not in danger. If it is a "darker" card or rune, I assume that there might be a problem, but the meaning of the individual rune or card must be taken into consideration.

Tea Leaves/Scrying

These two forms of divination suggest symbols to the mind that will trigger information to come forward from the psychic senses. Such divination techniques are very hard to use for yourself in terms of psychic self-defense, because they are the techniques most likely to be clouded by your subconscious thoughts and fears.

Egg Divination

I was taught this type of divination by a South American practitioner, specifically for diagnosing and healing illness, but it can also be used to diagnose harmful spirits and energies. It is much like the suggested imagery found in reading tea leaves or scrying in crystals. You take a fresh, raw egg, and have the person sit and reflect on their life and problem while holding the egg to their heart. Then crack the egg open and drop it into a fancy glass goblet filled with some water.

Gaze into the egg and yolk to determine if there is an outside force working against the person or an illness in the body, using the symbols suggested in the egg yolk. It is a very intuitive and difficult technique to explain; it simply must be experienced and improved upon with practice. I use this technique when people come to me believing they have been cursed.

Malocchio

Malocchio means "evil eye" and comes from the Italian folk magick traditions. The cure for the malocchio is one of the most powerful forms of diagnosis and curse breaking, even if the source of harm is not one versed in Italian magick. I learned this cure from my mother, who learned it from her family. Her godmother was the "curse breaker" of the Italian community of her town. Traditionally, the knowledge is passed on Christmas Eve. The technique is both a divination of the evil eye and a breaking of it. There are many forms of this ritual. This is the form I learned and pass on to you now.

You will need a needle, some extra virgin olive oil, and a cooking pot for spaghetti. Bring the water to a boil, and then reduce the heat to low and let it simmer. Put three drops of oil in the water. If the oil separates, smears, or mixes, then the malocchio is not present. If the oil drops come together, then the evil eye is present. My mother gazes into the dance of the oil in water like others look into crystal balls or mirrors, and divines even more information about the curse. To break the curse, sterilize the needle in an open flame from a candle you have blessed. Then take the needle and plunge it into the oil, breaking it apart. We originally learned a Christian prayer to Jesus and Mary, but I now say, "Eye against eye, I ask the Goddess and God to break this curse. So mote it be." If the oil does not break with the first motion of the needle, repeat until it does. The more difficult the break, the stronger the evil eye is.

Aura Gazing

Those versed in aura gazing can often tell if a person has an unhealthy energy directed or attached to them. Those truly gifted in the art of aura gazing may even pick up very specific information about where the energy came from, who it came from, if applicable, and what it is doing on the mental, emotional, and physical levels. Even if you are skilled at aura gazing, it is a difficult technique to use for yourself. You can try looking in the mirror. For more on aura gazing, read my book *The Inner Temple of Witchcraft: Magick, Meditation and Psychic Development*.

Shamanic Journey

Shamanic journey is my favorite form of divination, but again it is another technique that is hard to use for yourself. It consists of entering a trance state with your questions in mind, visiting the shamanic otherworlds, and seeking counsel from the spirit world. It takes an experienced practitioner to come back with definitive answers, but such answers will contain a great deal of symbolic information.

There was one time when I felt the need to consult a shamanic practitioner for answers regarding another practitioner. I had a sneaky suspicion that this person wished me harm, but had nothing on which to base it. I had a few of the classic symptoms of psychic attack, from sudden pains and unexpected illness to a series of misfortunes, but I was in denial and sought other explanations without giving this person serious consideration. Then some mutual acquaintances came into my life again and confirmed that this person had strong feelings against me and had been known to do harmful magick before. I still couldn't believe it, and chalked it up to community gossip.

Finally, I was in the company of a shamanic practitioner and given the opportunity to have her do a journey for me. She said to think of my question, but not to say it out loud. When she returned from the trance, she described the suspected person's personality very well. This person was embodied as a scorpion at my throat fighting my spirit totem, a spider. The spider was losing because I was not cheering it on and honoring it for protecting me. She removed the scorpion and its poison, and healed my throat. I'm sure the practitioner who caused me harm didn't use shamanism or even any scorpion imagery, but that is how it appeared symbolically to my shamanic practitioner. My problems started to clear up, and I became much more diligent in my own psychic self-defense rituals.

The next day, I saw two other shamanic practitioners who were taking a Tarot course I was teaching. They both took me aside after class and said that I looked like a great weight had been lifted off me. I seemed clear and free and healthier than I had been in weeks. The diagnosis and healing had a real effect that others noticed too.

CHAPTER 3

PSYCHIC HYGIENE

Prevention is the best medicine, and I feel that issues of psychic defense are often much like illness. Things are out of balance and need to be brought back into harmony. If you can prevent things from throwing you off balance, you are better off. Holistic magick helps you bolster your own strength so you won't be knocked off your center during times of stress, when you are more vulnerable to illness. Basic forms of psychic care, or hygiene, when done regularly, give you this magickal immunity to most forms of harm.

The wonderful thing about these psychic hygiene techniques is that they are available to anyone who wants to use them. They require no special talents or developed magickal abilities other than a willingness to try. I teach them to friends, family, students, and clients.

SPIRITUAL BODIES

Just like we maintain proper hygiene and care of our physical bodies, we must do the same for our energy bodies. We prevent unhealthy forms of physical bacteria from accumulating and infecting our physical bodies, and we consume life-giving substances to keep the "motors" of our physical body going. We must do the same for our spiritual bodies. Just as our day-to-day actions get our physical bodies dirty, our day-to-day experiences do the same on the energetic level.

Most people in the modern world believe we have only one body. Some acknowledge an invisible presence animating that body. Most mainstream religions refer to this animating force as the soul. When a person dies, the soul leaves the body, and the body is no longer animated. It loses that vital spark and returns to the earth.

Wise ones from traditions all across the globe know this model is accurate, but very simplified. We actually have many different bodies, not just a physical body and soul. We are a unique blend of energies, of subtle bodies. In this lifetime and after death, some of these bodies separate and return to their source. In some belief systems, and with most modern witches, the individual sparks of life continue to another destination or future incarnation.

Metaphysicians have different ways of categorizing these energy bodies and have different names for them. Some systems have seven, nine, ten, or twelve bodies, each with various attributes. Even with so many differences, there are striking similarities. I think the discrepancies are caused by different points of view from both cultural and trained expectations. If you learn from a teacher or tradition that there are definitively twelve spiritual bodies, then in your experience, you will find twelve. If you are told there are seven, you will find seven. We often accede to the voice of authority and tradition.

In truth, I think the energy bodies are like the layers of water in the ocean. Science can describe the various layers of water in terms of pressure, temperature, light, current, and inhabitants, but it's hard to say where one level begins and another ends. A line is drawn at certain numbers, but those lines are fairly arbitrary. One level really flows into another, but we use these different features to differentiate them.

In magick, we do the same thing. We experience and measure different energy bodies, but they are all part of one great system, one great ocean that is flowing together and connected. The lines we draw are based on experience, but can be considered arbitrary. Just like pressure and temperature, psychic vibration is on a spectrum, with one level flowing into another. One spiritual body flows into and interpenetrates the others. The health of each body is dependent on the health of the other bodies. Changes in one body flow through and affect all the others, from the most subtle to the denser levels and back again.

To keep things simple, for this work we will be using a four-body system based on the four elements (figure 2). With knowledge of the four-body system, you can see how more complex systems of spiritual bodies, regardless of the name or culture, can usually be boiled down to these four bodies. Each body has specific needs and methods of care and cleansing.

Each element gives its own blessings and techniques for cleansing, healing, and balance. Each element offers its own path to psychic hygiene that can be used on a variety of levels. The elemental-hygiene techniques overlap in purpose and execution, since the spiritual bodies overlap. You may resonate with one technique more than another, and use it in all aspects. Only you can determine what techniques work best for you. The ones you will actually use are the ones you should focus on. If you know you will never take a ritual bath because you don't like baths, don't feel that you have to take one. Find at least one technique that works for you, and use it often.

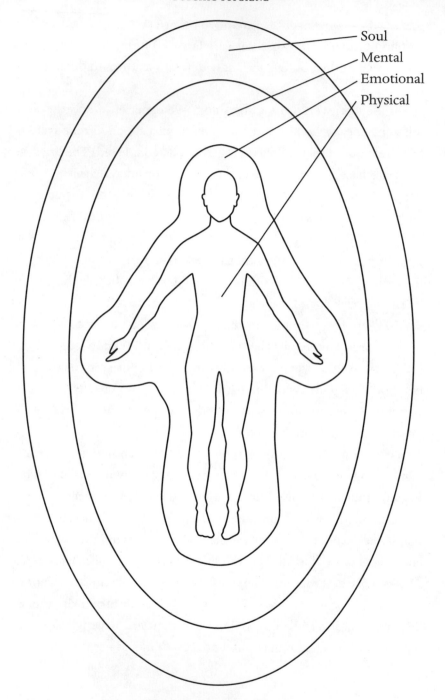

Soul
Mental
Emotional
Physical

Figure 2: Elements and Bodies

PHYSICAL BODY

The physical body is the one with which you are probably most familiar. It is the body of flesh and blood, organs and bone. The physical body relates to the element of earth, the densest of the four elements. Hopefully you have found physical hygiene techniques that work for you and the culture in which you live. Different parts of the world have different beliefs in the frequency and standards of bathing and scent. If you don't conform to them, I'm sure sooner or later someone will tell you.

When I talk about spiritually cleansing the physical body, I refer to the most dense and powerful techniques of cleansing. They are the most earthy. They involve physical action and simple ritual, and can have the most far-reaching effects on all the spiritual bodies. The simple ritual I find most powerful, and do almost daily, is the act of smudging.

Anyone can smudge, even if you do not "believe" in it. The cleansing effect is automatic, even if you do it without ceremony or intention. Saying you don't believe in the power of smudge is like saying you don't believe in the power of soap. If you use it properly, it will still work, even if you don't admit it. Just like soap, anyone can use incense.

Now, I know what some of you experienced pagans are saying: "Smudging uses incense. Incense is a tool of air. Wouldn't this be a technique for the mental, air body rather than the physical, earth body?" You are absolutely right. I understand your feelings, and technically, you could put smudging with air, or even with fire, because you light the incense with fire first, but I put it with earth for two reasons.

First, if you just do it, it will work. Smudging involves a simple physical action. For the air element, we will discuss more mental techniques, rather than simple physical actions. Anyone, and I mean anyone, can smudge. I've taught it to very non-mystically oriented people, and they have loved it.

Second, the substances we burn, the various herbs, woods, and resins, come from the natural realm. They come from the earth. Though nature is different from pure elemental earth energy in the strictest sense, they are in harmony with the element of earth.

Smudging is the ritual of passing yourself, others, or objects through the sacred smoke of a blessed incense. The smoke energetically purifies and cleanses. To cleanse a space, you can burn the incense in the area you wish to be purified. To purify an entire home or building, take the burning incense from room to room. Smudging works on a variety of levels. On the physical level, it changes the scent of the area. Humans respond to scent very strongly. Energies are associated with scent.

On a spiritual level, each substance used as incense has a specific vibration. When burned, that vibration is intensified and released into the space via the smoke, but emanates much further than the visible smoke. When the incense is blessed, the process is further intensified. The trick to formulating a strong cleansing and protective incense, what is otherwise called temple or sacred-space incense, is using substances that have strong, "high" vibrations, which are usually accompanied by a strong scent.

When people talk about "negative" energy, or what I call harmful or dense energy, since all energy is on a spectrum, they are talking about lower, slower, more stagnant energies. When you burn a powerfully protective and cleansing incense, its high vibration forces the other vibrations to match it or to be removed from the area. They can't exist at that lower, dense level when all the energy around them is being refined. A student once compared this process to the entrainment of clocks, where numerous clocks, all slightly out of phase, eventually come to the same pattern. If you have a stronger, louder clock, it could dominate the entrainment process. Energy works in a similar way, and the higher energy entrains the lower energy to match it. If it can't, it must leave the sacred space.

Various substances are used in the act of smudging, but not all incenses have the qualities of purification, banishment, and protection. Just because you like a particular incense doesn't mean it's always the proper one for smudging. Some incenses alter moods, add energy for spell work, attract love or money, induce trance, or celebrate an astrological, planetary, elemental, or seasonal energy. They are all great for their own purposes, but are not necessarily what you want for this work. Here are some tried-and-true protective and cleansing substances:

Sage: The favorite choice of Native American healers. There are many kinds of sage, including garden sage, sage brush, and California white sage, my personal favorite. All have similar properties.

Cedar and Sweet Grass: Both are from the American traditions. They can be used separately, together, or with sage.

Frankincense & Myrrh: This is the incense of choice for both witches and the Catholic church. Frankincense has a masculine quality of both the Sun and Jupiter, while myrrh has a feminine, lunar, and Saturn quality. When burned together, they create sacred space and banish unwanted influences.

Copal: Copal is a resin burned by Central and South American shamans, with strong protective qualities.

Lavender: Lavender is one of the most versatile herbs. Its wonderful, relaxing scent can be used to cleanse and protect a space.

Dragon's Blood: Dragon's blood is a red resin that acts as a power enhancer in any mixture. Burned alone, it holds the power of the warrior, ruled by Mars, and forcibly banishes unwanted spirits and energies.

Cinnamon: This aromatic spice, which is often used in cooking, can be burned to protect the home.

Cloves: Cloves are another herb of protection. Whole cloves are used as a safe substitute for "protection spikes," usually nails, pins, tacks, and glass called for in traditional protection spells, but when burned on a hot coal or in a fire, they release strong vibrations to clear out unwanted energies.

Mugwort: Traditionally known as a visionary and magickal herb, mugwort can also be used to banish unwanted energies and spirits when burned. My herbal teacher taught me how to make smudge wands by bundling mugwort together with other herbs such as sage, pine, cedar, sweet fern, or lavender. Mugwort is used in acupuncture sessions because it stimulates the flow of healthy energy, and traditionally is said to banish the energy of illness.

Pine: Pine, particularly white pine, holds a powerful protection of the god force. Each "leaf" bundle contains five needles, like a five-pointed flower. Such flowers often possess the power of protection attributed to the pentacle (see chapter 4). Pine makes an excellent incense to invoke the protective powers of the god force, ruled by both the Sun and Jupiter. It is often burned near the winter solstice in honor of the new God.

Sweet Fern: Sweet fern is a magickally diverse plant. It is used most often to soothe skin irritations and poison ivy. I learned to use it to repel insects. When burned, it is used to repel all unwanted pests and energies. Sweet fern works well with mugwort and juniper.

How to Smudge

Incense is available in wand, cone, stick, or granular form. Smudge wands are bundles of dried herbs packed together. Although available commercially, they are fun to make. Gather fresh herbs and lay them together. Wrap them tightly with cotton string, and allow them to dry on a screen so they get air evenly. Then light the tip and blow it out. Let the plants smoke and smolder, creating your sacred smoke. Have a flameproof vessel available to hold under the smudge stick. Some people use an earthen bowl or seashell.

Powdered incense is the messiest but most witchy! Grind your herbs to a powder using a traditional mortar and pestle or an electric grinder. Then get some charcoal blocks or discs, sold at most New Age stores, to use as your combustible base. Light the charcoal and sprinkle the incense on it to burn, adding more incense occasionally if you need more smoke. Using a nonflammable utensil, brush off the accumulated ash and add more herb. Start with single plants for now. You will learn to make a more complicated mixture in chapter 7.

Once the incense is smoking, pass whatever objects you are clearing through the smoke. If smudging yourself or another person, waft the smoke all over yourself. If possible, do the front and back.

Feathers are often used with traditional sage wands or other herb bundles. A feather, such as a turkey or crow feather, is used to fan the embers and make more smoke.

Smudging can be a ceremony. I often hold the burning incense to the north, east, south, west, above, below near the ground, my left side, right side, and then my heart, asking for the blessing of all the directions and the gods, before smudging myself, someone else, or an object. If you work with specific deities, totems, or angels (see chapter 6), you can call upon them as a part of your personal cleansing ritual. Be creative in your smudging rituals.

To truly protect the physical body, be aware and present in your body. Center yourself through rituals like smudging. Those who are aware can react more effectively to difficult situations.

EMOTIONAL BODY

The emotional body is symbolized by the element of water. This body has many names to it. Some call it the emotional body, while others call it the astral body, psychic body, or dream body. Each one has a different cultural connotation, but they all have similar energies.

This plane of energy is symbolized by water because it flows and takes shape, like water in a vessel. The force of will and imagination gives shape and form to this astral energy. When we sleep and connect with the astral plane, our thoughts, from our daily life to our hopes, dreams, and fears, take shape on the astral plane. We experience them as dreams. Our emotions also take on shape and form by our will and imagination. They flow and change easily. Like water, they can be clear and cool, or turbulent and choppy.

Water is particularly susceptible to pollution. Water flows freely into or over all things, picking up impurities along the way. The same thing can happen with our emotions. Without a strong sense of boundary to our emotional body, we take on emotional pollutants and toxins from other people and places. Because water energy is considered to be a psychic energy, the emotional body is often the energetic realm where we take in psychic information. Without strong psychic boundaries, it is hard to tell what is a true psychic impression, an insight or message, and what is a false impression created from our own personal desires and fears or from the psychic pollutants we take on from others. When we can't tell the difference, we take on emotions and impressions from others. Without recognizing what is happening, we cannot stop it.

Awareness of Others

Empathy is the ability to feel another's emotions and relate to their point of view. Most non-magickal practitioners think of it symbolically, as an intellectual understanding of another's feelings. Magickal practitioners realize that emotions are energy, and to be empathic can be a great gift or a great difficulty, depending on how it is expressed and handled.

Empathy is a blessing when you are solid in your own personal foundation and use your sensitivity to gain greater awareness of relationships and situations. When communicating with another, it is very important to be sensitive to the person's feelings. Empathy gives us a way to communicate beyond words. Communication mediums that lack emotional resonance, such as computers, can confuse empathic people.

In a sense, we are all empathic. We all pick up on the energy of tone, inflection, and implied emotion. There are simply levels of sensitivity. People who consider themselves empathic have this ability in a greater range than the rest of the general population. Those with healthy empathy often become healers, teachers, therapists, social workers, artists, performers, and musicians. These vocations all require a developed level of sensitivity. They are also jobs with a high burn-out rate, because many people have the sensitivity, but lack the grounding and boundaries needed to maintain long-term health.

Empathy is also somewhat of a curse when it is uncontrolled. Some people are easily overwhelmed by other people's emotions and energy, not knowing where their own feelings begin and end. Other empaths are not overwhelmed, but feel they are so skilled in the emotional realm of water that they never really learn how to use the element of air to express their feelings, so other people have a hard time relating to them.

Early on, such sensitive souls assume everyone has the same level of awareness that they do, and they feel hurt when they are misunderstood. On the other hand, these empaths don't learn to listen to other people's words. They feel the emotions, but ignore the rest of the communication. Sometimes the emotions are truer, but when a person with less empathy feels like they are being "read" and not listened to, it can cause a lot of complications.

In the same vein, some people are not receptive empaths, but projecting empaths. Although the two often go hand in hand, some projecting empaths are oblivious to other people's emotions, but strongly broadcast their own moods and affect everybody else around them. This is not necessarily a bad thing. Such empaths can project joy, love, and peace, as well as nervousness, depression, and anger. Their mood becomes the dominant feeling in the area, and most people don't understand why.

The next time you are in an environment with other people and find your mood suddenly shift, be aware of the others around you. Say, for example, that you are at a party and suddenly find your mood shifting for no reason, or shifting somewhat out of character. Take a look around the room and see if you find anyone with a similar mood or temperament. If you do, acknowledge it and put out the intention to be balanced and centered. Notice if your mood shifts back to a more expected mode.

Uncontrolled empathy is an issue of boundaries, of being able to turn on abilities when needed, but also to be able to turn down sensitivity or projection when overwhelming. The boundary and healing techniques in this section, when practiced diligently, are very helpful for those with strong empathy issues. Regular, disciplined meditation and ritual of an introspective nature is very helpful as well.

Without these practices, it can be hard to discern which feelings are coming from an outside source and which are your own. In times of crisis, it is easy to dismiss deep feelings that arise and are in need of healing, and rationalize that they are the emotions of others. Likewise, projecting empaths who become aware of their abilities are often martyrs who do not go out and socialize because they are afraid of hurting others. When you have difficulty with personal boundaries, it is easy to blame others or accept all the blame. The truth lies somewhere in the middle.

Ultimately empathy is a great teacher and a great gift. It is not always easy, but those who face its challenges are called to deep lessons of psychic awareness.

Ritual Bathing

One of the best cleansing and healing techniques of the emotional body is ritual bathing. The purifying power of water is not to be underestimated. Many traditions of witchcraft talk about the necessity of a ritual bath before any serious working, but most witches I know skip the bath and go straight for the spells. When you do a ritual bath, there is something more charged, more magickal, and more magnetic about the ritual, so I don't skip it unless I'm short on time.

Water cleanses the emotional body and releases emotional toxins while at the same time cleansing the physical body. Many of the herbs of protection and cleansing are also used in ritual baths to infuse the water with their properties. Salts are also used, since salts magickally draw out dense energies. Vinegar is also used to neutralize harmful energies. Vinegar can be left in a bowl to absorb and collect these energies, and then dumped out into the earth or down a drain. Vinegar can also be used in cleansing baths. I have a friend who learned to take a "beer bath," what was traditionally a barley water bath, to shed unwanted influences, particularly when he felt he was under psychic attack. Vinegar and beer baths don't always smell great, so I prefer this formula.

Cleansing Bath Salt

1 cup sea salt (you can use Epsom salt if you prefer, but I prefer the healing properties of sea salt)

1 tablespoon lavender flowers/leaves

½ tablespoon yarrow flowers/leaves

1 pinch mugwort or myrrh

5 drops lavender essential oil

3 drops myrrh essential oil

As you mix these ingredients together, hold each one in your hands (except the oils) and feel your energy mingle with it, drawing out its natural healing powers. Ask the blessing of the Goddess and God to protect and cleanse you. Mix all the ingredients together and let the mixture sit in an airtight bottle for a few weeks to allow the scents to mingle. Place a few tablespoons of the mixture in a muslin or cotton bag in your bath water. You can even tie it over the faucet. Bathe in the water, and when you are ready to get out, let the water drain while you sit in the tub, allowing it to take the unwanted energies down the drain, to be cleansed and neutralized with the salt and herbs.

Floral Waters

Another method of protection with water is the use of herbal and floral waters. Rose water is the most common and powerful of such waters. Rose water can be bought at many drug stores, but you can also make it at home. An easy method is to put a few drops of rose essential oil in a solution of 75 percent water and 25 percent alcohol (to preserve) and shake it up. The number of drops is up to you, depending on the strength of scent you prefer. This is not a true rose water, but it is magickally effective. This method can be expensive if you use genuine rose oil rather than the cheaper synthetic oils, but synthetic oils do not carry any magick in them. There are several grades of quality for genuine rose essential oil, so you can find a cheaper variety.

The next method of making rose water is the easiest. Make a tea infusion of rose petals and water. Place one tablespoon of rose petals in one cup of boiling water for about fifteen minutes. Then mix it with the water and alcohol solution. I use vodka, because it lasts the longest as a preservative, but if you don't like it, you can use vegetable glycerin.

The third technique involves creating a true hydrosol (figure 3). Get a big pot that is not aluminum, and two smaller bowls that will fit in the pot. Place one bowl upside-down as a stand, and place the other bowl right-side up on top of the first bowl. This second bowl will "catch" the liquid that is brewed. Put rose petals and just enough water to cover them in the bottom of the pot, and place the cover of the pot on the pot, upside-down. Hopefully your cover will come to a point, with its handle pointing downward toward the upright bowl. Heat the mixture. Water will evaporate from the bottom of the pot, collect on the top cover, and trickle down into the upright bowl. The water collected in the bowl is your rose water, also known as rose hydrosol. Preserve it with some alcohol or glycerin. Rose water is also available commercially as a cosmetic in local health food stores and drug stores. Read the label to make sure the rose water is made from natural roses and not synthetic oil.

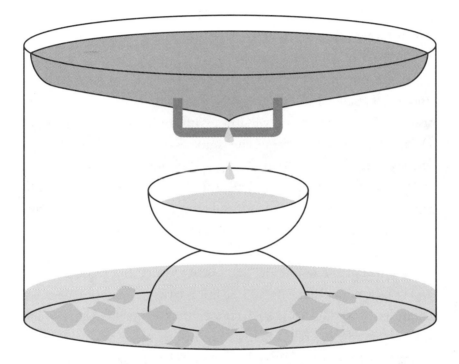

Figure 3: Rose Hydrosol

Commercial hydrosols are usually a by-product of essential oil distillation, but the homemade method can be fun to experiment with. I actually prefer the results of the commercial waters in terms of scent quality, but enjoy making my own products.

Roses are both spiritually uplifting and grounded. They are the vibration of pure love, and the most protective substance in many traditions. The flower is love, but the thorns are protection. If you can't use rose water or rose oil, try visualizing roses around you for protection. Invite in the spirit of the rose flower. They will wilt in your mind's eye as they absorb harmful energy. Then move the rose images out of your area and imagine them dissolving in flame, purifying the energy as you grow new psychic roses.

Roses are not the only protective plant you can use. Witch hazel extract is also very protective and commercially available, although not as lovely smelling. You can make infusions of any of the protective herbs. Use your imagination.

Bless your herbal water with the intention of protection. Then anoint yourself with it on the pulse points and chakras. Trace the frames of your doors and windows with the water. I usually move clockwise around the frame, but some witches associate counterclockwise movement with protection. You can put a floral water in a spray bottle, and spray away harmful vibrations in your rooms. In chapter 7, you will learn the formula for a more intense protective and banishing spray using floral waters and essential oils.

The nature of the emotional body is like water and can easily mix and mingle with others. As we lose boundaries, sometimes we make connections to others and such connections create an inappropriate flow of energy. We take energy from others or let others take our energy, creating harmful psychic cords. We are linked through our emotional body, and through various chakras. When someone can "pull your strings," they are literally pulling your energy, creating a reaction in the emotional body. To learn how to break such cords, call upon the angelic realm, as described in chapter 6.

MENTAL BODY

The mental body is probably the body that needs cleansing the most. Most minds are a jumbled clutter, so it takes serious effort to find and use the things we place in our mind without tripping over all the accumulated waste of our years. Much of the spiritual process is about getting our mental closets free of excess, and finding a sense of simple order and harmony.

We have millions of thoughts a day, but each day we repeat the majority of those thoughts. We continue stagnant patterns, following what is familiar, and do not create anything new. Energy flows from the most primal levels to the dense levels to manifest. Our thoughts are less dense, and they create feelings. Emotions are denser than thoughts. If you focus on a particular thought long enough, you will begin to conjure feelings associated with it. Try thinking about a particularly painful or joyous time in your life, and notice how your thoughts manifest actual feelings. Feelings create sensations, bodily reactions measurable in the physical world. The physical world is more dense than the emotional world. While reflecting on your painful/joyous experience, notice how your breathing patterns, heartbeat, and muscle contractions change. Strong emotions can bring tears. Difficult emotions usually bring a contraction and quickening, while pleasurable emotions bring release. The health of the mind creates the health in the emotional and physical levels.

The true innovators and magickal personalities are those who can think outside of the usual patterns and habits to see things differently. If we truly want to use our mental body, we must exercise it like our physical body. Our mental exercises are not simply actions of math and memorization found in traditional schoolwork. Although helpful, they are not the most powerful techniques, because they, too, can trap you in patterns. Mental cleansing is not learning to think in the way everyone else thinks, but finding the true self. The most mentally cleansing experiences are those that release what does not serve in the mind, and help train the mind to be your tool, servant, and aid, rather than your master, trapping you in its comfortable patterns. Mental introspection is the key.

Introspection brings awareness. We do so many things without being conscious of our actions. We do them out of habit. We hold on to the strong energy of past events and patterns, without even realizing it. Introspection reveals our patterns and allows us to decide which things serve us and which things may be contributing to the undesirable events in our life.

Journaling

If you have never done any introspective work before, I suggest starting with journaling. Write down the things in your life that are on your mind, but establish a discipline for your journaling. Don't just write what you want, whenever you feel like it.

I like the suggestion of Julia Cameron, author of *The Artist's Way: A Spiritual Path to Higher Creativity*. She recommends making a commitment to write three pages every day, no matter what. Even if all you can write is three pages of "I don't know what to write," do it. Eventually, you will start to write what is on your mind consciously, such as events of the day and your feelings and reactions to them, and then you will tap into the subconscious, and start writing about the patterns that are not as obvious. You can write three pages a day without delving into yourself. Cameron suggests writing "morning pages," but I find it easier to write before I go to bed. Journaling gives you an outlet to let go of many things.

Then, if you wait a few weeks or months and peruse your entries, you will see how much your feelings and thoughts have changed, and you will begin to recognize your reaction patterns and see your life themes. Journaling can be very challenging, but is worthwhile.

I also suggest keeping a dream journal, either separate from your regular journal, or as a part of it. Dream symbols help us reflect even more deeply on the unconscious themes manifested in our sleep. Dreaming is a great magickal time of discovery and healing.

Meditation

The next tool of mental hygiene is regular meditation. Meditation is taking time to go within and be quiet. There are many meditation techniques available, from Eastern techniques of watching the mind, focusing on the breath, or using a mantra, to Western visualization and relaxation techniques. Taking time regularly to go within, be quiet, and listen to your highest guidance, even if you don't get a message, helps clear out the mental patterns and gives you a fresh perspective. Regular meditation reduces stress and increases vitality and creativity. I definitely feel it when I let my daily meditation practice slide. I'm not as healthy, aware, happy, and vital. Some people meditate for ten minutes a day, others for two hours, and anywhere in between. Just take the time and, like journaling, be disciplined about it. Make it a habit for twenty-eight days, the cycle of the Moon. Then see how easy it will be to keep the habit. For more in-depth techniques on meditation, read my book *The Inner Temple of Witchcraft: Magick, Meditation and Psychic Development*.

Therapy or Counseling

The last introspective technique for the air element and mental body is therapy or counseling. Most people balk at this suggestion, but such work is not just for people who are "sick." There is a stigma attached to it, even among witches, that people who need counseling are not normal or are somewhat deranged. We do not need to brand ourselves or anyone else with such labels. We all have difficult times in our lives, and we can all heal. When we need help going within, seeing our patterns, we should seek an outside, objective source. Though most people go to friends and family, which can be helpful, having a truly objective, unattached, trained person is very helpful in sorting out thoughts, feelings, and experiences. Don't feel embarrassed or ashamed when seeking outside counsel. In fact, it is a sign of a healthy, sane, balanced adult when you can admit that you need help.

SOUL BODY

The soul body relates to the fire element, that personal spark of the divine we all hold. The soul is associated with the highest level of spiritual knowing, often called the higher self. This is the body that is the most energetic and elusive, and therefore the most protected and untouchable from outside harm. Its fiery nature prevents much of our harmful energy from accumulating, burning away that which doesn't serve us. In our true essence, we are connected to all things, yet bound by none. By identifying with the soul, the divine, rather than with our mind, emotions, or body, we find true protection, fearlessness, and eternal wisdom.

Solar Spiritual Fire

The healing and protection techniques of fire extend divine energy from our soul into our other subtle bodies. The first technique uses solar fire to heal and protect. To get in touch with this solar fire directly, go outside into the sunlight. Sunlight can expand and cleanse the aura. This doesn't mean ritualistic sunbathing with magickal tanning lotions, but simply being outside and exposing yourself to the light for five to ten minutes a day. Let the spiritual energy of the sun burn away the harmful energies you have accumulated. Sunlight fills the aura with vital life energy, making you healthier and more resistant to harm on all levels. Some studies suggest that regular, moderate exposure to sunlight enhances the immune system directly.

The second technique echoes the first. Regularly visualize the Sun above you while in meditation, and imagine drawing down the golden white light of the Sun around you, surrounding you and revitalizing you. You can do this technique in deep meditation, but also when you are simply relaxing with your eyes closed. You don't have to be in a deep trance or perform an in-depth ritual to invite the healing energies of fire, light, and the Sun for health and protection.

Start thinking about yourself as existing on all four spiritual levels simultaneously. True health occurs on all of these levels, through balance and harmony with your physical, emotional, mental, and soul components. Mastery of these levels gives you all the spiritual protection you need.

CHAPTER 4

MARKED FOR PROTECTION

One of the most prevalent types of protection magick comes in the form of a magickal amulet. Amulets are traditionally used to grant the wearer any number of magickal abilities, but protection is one of the most sought-after powers. Such devices are found in all cultures and all religions. The desire for protection from harm, malice, or accident is universal. All people, ancient and modern, petition the divine in all manner of ways through the use of special symbols and jewelry to gain such protection. Evidence of protection charms dates back to the cradle of civilization, to the lands of Sumer and Egypt, although I'm sure if we could travel back to the Stone Age, we would find that our most ancient ancestors used various items for protection as well. Little evidence of these ancient Stone Age charms exists, but tribal cultures surviving into the modern era still use protection charms.

Protection charms have found their way into modern times. Believe it or not, such talismanic magick can be found right in the modern Christian churches. Those who wear a cross or crucifix as a sign of faith and for protection are using the symbol of the cross as a magickal device. My father used to travel extensively, and wore a St. Christopher medal, the patron saint of travelers. In some churches, there were special times when the priest would bless such jewelry. The idea of a cross or medal for protection being sanctioned by the Church is a vestige of old magick. In the Dark and Middle Ages, the Church warned people about the horrors of black magick and satanic witches that were lurking everywhere, sparking the witch hunts. Belief in supernatural creatures, such as demons, devils, imps, vampires, and werewolves, abounded as well. At the time, people believed that only the intervention of the divine, usually envisioned as the Christian father god, could save them. Such jewelry acted like touchstones, showing God where to look and whom to protect. The idea is the same as with many ancient pagan amulets of protection: they are petitions to invite the divine into your life for protection. Some symbols are specific to certain gods, while others evoke a general divine protection.

HOW DO PROTECTION CHARMS WORK?

Protection charms work through energy, vibration, and the intention behind the creation of the symbol or charm used. Symbols and talismans are a way to communicate your intention to the universe. The charm holds the intention, and its energy attracts or repels things in accordance with your wishes. They are very subtle in operation, and if you have a good protection amulet, your life will move so smoothly and safely that you will not even know you have it.

Unfortunately, many people believe that if they use a protection amulet, they will be impervious from all harm. A few stupid mistakes will hopefully cure them of such erroneous thinking, without too much damage to their body or pride. Some people think that you can wear a magickal charm and expect that a speeding truck will have no effect on you should you decide to step in front of it; but magickal protection doesn't grant you absolute invulnerability. That is Hollywood movie magick, and not really a part of real-world, practical magick. If you consciously and willingly put yourself in harm's way, then you will reap the consequences of your actions.

Magickal amulets will ward off harmful energies before they manifest physically in your life. The magick of such charms strengthens your own natural shields and defenses, strengthening your aura, your own natural boundary. They can create a barrier between you and any psychic harm. Often they will either ward off psychic "vampires" by creating an inhospitable vibration, or make you psychically "invisible" to their senses so they leave you alone. Such amulets will also bring a greater sense of intuitive awareness of potential danger on a psychic and physical level. With it, even if you don't consider yourself intuitive, you might have an intuitive flash to take a different route home or trust your instincts about a particular person; and in the end, these small decisions could save your life.

SYMBOLS OF PROTECTION

The symbols presented in this section have a tradition of being used for protection and divine blessings. Symbols work in the most amazing way. They are like codes to speak directly with the divine mind.

We, as humans, often have difficulty recognizing and using magickal energy in its raw form, so we attach symbols to our magickal intents. Symbols give our mind something to process. The symbols stand for the magick we are evoking.

Symbols also help us separate from our doubt. When we ask for something in words, through prayer or traditional spell work, we can become very attached to our desire, and not release the energy to let the magick manifest. Sometimes our attachment comes in the form of fear and doubt. We keep repeating our intention, but our doubts surface because the desired outcome is not yet a reality. Symbols provide us with a step between our desire and its manifestation, helping us distance ourselves from our own personal doubt and thus enabling us to create more effective magick.

Symbol magick can be divided into symbols that we have intellectually created with a specific magickal goal, and symbols we "receive" from a higher divine source. Most of the symbols used for protection are considered to be divine symbols, manifestations of the sacred geometry of life. They are touchstones to the gods, goddesses, and divine powers. When we wear these symbols, we are asking the divine powers to protect us.

One truly astounding fact about symbol magick is that their power builds up over time. If a symbol is used over and over again, with the same intent, it can carry a greater magickal "charge" to it. People over centuries of time have contributed to the power and intention behind that symbol. Their belief, will, and intent have contributed to the power you are carrying.

Pentagram

The pentagram is one of the most misunderstood symbols in the Western world. Many people associate it with Satanism, but its origins are ancient, predating any concept of the Devil. The five points are symbolic of the five elements, the five senses, and the human form. This sacred-geometry figure is a symbol of protection, a sacred shield. Pentagrams are gateways to open portals to new energies and spirits, or to close the door and banish energies. Warriors use this symbol on their shields. Witches wear pentagrams as a focus for magickal energy and protection both magickally and in daily life. The pentagram is the symbol of modern witchcraft, and most witches wear the pentagram in the form of a ring or necklace.

When you draw the banishing pentagram, you banish all harmful, unwanted energies. There are many types of banishing pentagrams, for each of the elements. The basic banishing pentagram, used for all protection purposes, corresponds with the earth element (figure 4). I visualize it in blue or violet light and draw it in all four directions around me, above me, and below me to cleanse the space and protect myself.

A pentagram in a circle is usually called a pentacle and can be used for protection just as easily as the pentagram.

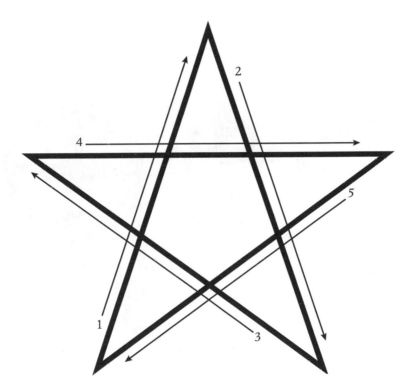

Figure 4: Banishing Pentagram

Figure 5: Ankh

Ankh

The ankh is the symbol of life and is often called the Egyptian cross. This powerful image is symbolic of the union of the goddess Isis and her husband/brother Osiris, the mother and father gods of Egypt.

Figure 6: Christian Cross, Celtic Cross, Earth Cross

Cross

The cross is a powerful symbol of protection and is used most often by Christians as a symbol of their faith and belief in Jesus Christ. I know Christian witches, or those who identify as Christian but do ritual magick, who use the cross and crucifix in their ceremonies for protection and blessing. Many pagans identify with the Celtic cross, an extended cross with a loop around it, associated with the early Celtic Christian church. Most pagans look to the equal-armed cross, in or out of a circle, as a symbol of protection and of Mother Earth. The four arms are like the four directions of the world and the four elements of the magick circle. Any of these crosses can be worn for protection.

Figure 7: Eye of Horus

Eye of Horus

The Eye of Horus is another Egyptian symbol that is now used for protection. It is associated with Horus, the son of Isis and Osiris, though some call it the Eye of Ra, the creator sun god. Horus' eyes are said to be the Sun and Moon, and he is considered to be a great protector and avenging warrior god.

Figure 8: Hexagram

Hexagram

The hexagram is a six-pointed star. It is often referred to as the Star of David in Judaism, but can be found in many other esoteric systems as well. It represents many things: the forces above and below meeting in the center, the four elements, the four directions, and also the directions of above and below. The hexagram is often used as a symbol for the heart chakra, representing the union of the force above with the forces below, in the place of balance and unconditional love. It is also the symbol of the celestial sphere, representing the six magickal planets of the Moon, Mercury, Venus, Mars, Jupiter, and Saturn, with the Sun in the center. Many use the hexagram for balanced protection, particularly if they fear the five-pointed pentagram.

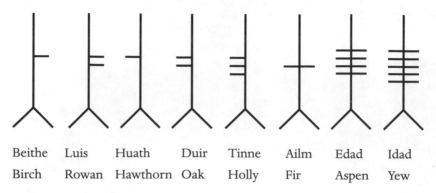

Beithe	Luis	Huath	Duir	Tinne	Ailm	Edad	Idad
Birch	Rowan	Hawthorn	Oak	Holly	Fir	Aspen	Yew

Figure 9: Protection Ogham

Ogham

The ogham alphabet is a Celtic symbol system associated with trees. Used both for divination and communication and, as some modern scholars argue, a calendar, certain oghams are used for protection. The symbols pictured here can be creatively fashioned into amulets for protection.

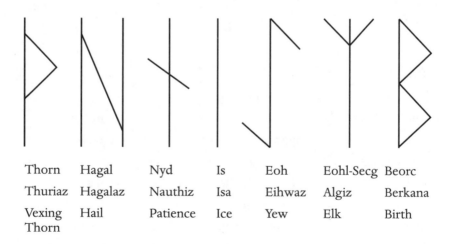

Thorn	Hagal	Nyd	Is	Eoh	Eohl-Secg	Beorc
Thuriaz	Hagalaz	Nauthiz	Isa	Eihwaz	Algiz	Berkana
Vexing Thorn	Hail	Patience	Ice	Yew	Elk	Birth

Figure 10: Protection Runes

Runes

The runes are a Norse magick symbol system used for divination and spellcraft. Runes were carved into tools and talismans to bring blessings. You can wear the runes pictured here for protection.

Figure 11: Thor's Hammer

Thor's Hammer

This symbol is attributed to Thor, the Norse god of thunder and lightning, and a champion and protector of the common man. It is used by many Norse pagans for guidance and protection.

Figure 12: Triple Knot

Triple Knot

A variety of triple knot and triple-pronged symbols are used for protection (figures 12–14). Such symbols are said to confuse and bind harmful energy, since it cannot easily follow the pattern in the knot or spirals. Usually attributed to a Celtic source, they are symbols of protection used by witches as symbols of the Triple Goddess. Witches who are not comfortable with the pentacle, publicly or privately, will use the triple figure in place of the five-pointed star.

Figure 13: Triple Spiral

Figure 14: Triskallion

To use these symbols of protection, you can often find them crafted into jewelry. Some are more esoteric and not easily available. You can draw the symbol on wood, clay, stone, or even paper and carry it with you as an amulet.

STONES OF PROTECTION

Rocks, minerals, and crystals are traditional vessels for magickal intention. Each stone carries its own unique spirit and power based on its color, composition, and historic use. In Western magick, crystals with a dark, rich color, such as black, brown, deep red, and deep green, have very strong protective powers. Stones associated with the elements of earth and fire, and the planets Saturn, Mars, and the Earth, are stones of protection. Practitioners of other systems of magick believe that certain stones are sacred to different deities, and that if you want to gain the protection of a specific deity, you use that deity's sacred stone, symbol, or object.

The following stones, minerals, metals, and fossils have all been used for protection, among other uses. Each one has a different personality, so pick the ones you are drawn to use.

Amber
Flourite
Garnet
Hematite
Iron
Jade
Jasper, Red
Jet
Lead
Malachite
Onyx
Quartz
Smokey Quartz
Tourmaline
Tourmalated Quartz
Turquoise

Before using a stone as a protective amulet, cleanse it. Smudge it with your clearing incense or leave it in the sunlight for a few hours. Then meditate with the stone and ask the stone spirit for help and protection. Place your intention of protection into the stone. Empower the stone with your thoughts and magick.

Stones can be combined with symbols. If the idea appeals to you, try drawing protective symbols with paint, marker, or even carefully dripped candle wax onto your stone. Some shops sell stones with symbols already carved into them. Unless you are well versed in stone cutting, it's a hard trick to do at home. Polished crystals can be hard to draw on, but you can get a black or white stone at a river or beach, and use it as your base for further symbol magick. If you feel intuitively that the stone is powerful and its spirit is willing to be a protector and help evoke protective energies, then use it. Don't limit yourself to this list of stones.

HERBS OF PROTECTION

Herbs also play an important part in protection magick. Certain herbs were worn as charms, or sprinkled around a building, to ward off both physical and spiritual harm. The powers of protective herbs have made their way into our popular folklore. For example, everyone knows to use garlic for protection against unwanted vampires. Although this seems like a superstition, its root comes from our knowledge of the powerful protective properties of garlic. Garlic not only protects us spiritually, but it also stimulates the immune system to protect us against illness.

Most traditional herbal lore has few applications, since those living in more mystical times were predominately concerned about basic life needs—love, prosperity, healing, and protection. Most herbs used magickally have some protective elements, whether they are used to protect you from direct harm, center your energy, bring guidance to avoid harm, strengthen self-preservation intuition, or create a magickal boundary. Although all the herbs listed here are protection herbs, each has an individual personality or flair that must be explored and partnered with. Through your own use, discover how the protection herbs differ.

All the herbs used in protective and purifying incenses that were listed in chapter 3 would also be included in this category, along with these additional herbs:

Agrimony
Alder
Aloe

Amaranthus

Angelica

Anise Seed

Ash

Basil

Bay

Belladonna

Betony

Birch

Blackberry

Bloodroot

Boneset

Broom

Caraway

Cinnamon

Cinquefoil

Comfrey

Coriander

Daisy

Dill

Dragon's Blood

Elder

Fennel

Foxglove

Frankincense

Garlic

Ginger

Ginseng

Hawthorn

Juniper

Lavender

Loosestrife, Purple

Mandrake

Marigold

Mistletoe

Motherwort

Mugwort

Mullein

Myrrh

Nettle

Nightshade

Oak

Pine

Poke

Quince

Rose

Rosemary

Rowan

Rue

Sage

Sandalwood

Solomon's Seal

St. John's Wort

Star Anise

Sunflower

Thistle

Thyme

Tobacco

Yarrow

Vervain

Vinca

Violet

Willow

Witch Hazel

Wolf's Bane (Monkshood)

Wormwood

Yew

One of the most renowned protection herbs is moly. Moly is the mystical herb of the Greek god Hermes, who gave it to Odysseus to ward off the spells of Circe. It is known as the cure-all for evil magick. Unfortunately, there is great debate as to what moly really is, or if it was a real physical herb at all, since descriptions of it vary. No one is absolutely sure what moly is under our modern system of botanical names. Folk names varied from place to place. Modern witches sometimes relate the great powers of moly either to true European mandrake or to rue.

If you decide to make an herbal charm, carry a small quantity of the herb with you. People usually carry herbal charms in a small bag or sachet in a color that matches their spiritual intention. For protection magick, you can use white, black, brown, dark green, red, or turquoise. If the herb or herbs you are using have a flower that matches one of these colors, think about using that color for your herbal charm bag. If you want to be really fancy, the vessel for your herbs could be a glass or metal vial, a small wooden box, or a leather pouch.

Place one to three tablespoons of the herb in your container. The ideal time to do this is at the waning Moon, close to the New Moon but before the Moon enters the first quarter and begins to wax. If you can harvest the fresh plant and say prayers to it, making a petition for its protective powers before you harvest it, the charm will be even more powerful. If you can't obtain the herb locally, sit and meditate with the dried, purchased herb before you use it. Ask the plant spirit's permission and infuse your intention of protection into the herb as you place it in the vessel. Then carry it with you for protection.

You will learn to combine herbal magick with stones and symbols in chapter 7. Natural substances and symbols work quite well together for protection.

CHAPTER 5

BECOMING A PSYCHIC BLACK BELT

Imagine you are a tree. Your roots are deep and strong, digging down into the earth, anchoring you in the soil. Feel your trunk rise high and your many branches sway in the wind. Although you are anchored, as the great wind rises, you are flexible. Your branches and trunk move easily with the winds, bending, never breaking, and yet you never lose your roots.

Those skilled in the art of psychic defense live life like a tree, particularly when faced with difficulties; they are grounded and centered, yet flexible and adapting when facing life's trials. Think of how many people and situations blow through your life like a strong wind, knocking things down, and then just as quickly blow right out. One without a foundation will be yanked up and tossed around. One who stands inflexible will eventually be broken. Only with roots and flexibility will you survive the storms of life.

Like the growth of a tree, such psychic development is lifelong work. Some people naturally have strong roots, and some people naturally have flexibility; but developing both, and a myriad of other protection skills, takes a lifetime of learning and practice. Psychic protection is like a martial art in that it takes time to practice and develop your skills. No matter now much you know, you can always go deeper with your experience. And like martial artists, who are true warriors, spiritual warriors and guardians do not initiate violence, but rather they keep the peace. At its heart, psychic protection is an art of defense, not offense.

ELEMENTAL APPROACH TO PSYCHIC DEFENSE

By continuing to use the five elements as our guide to a balanced path, we receive five very different gifts:

> Earth = Grounding
>
> Water = Boundary
>
> Air = Flexibility
>
> Fire = Action
>
> Spirit = Compassion

Each is a path to protection, but I have found that being versed in all five gives you the greatest ability to deal with difficult situations. Many teachings will focus on just one aspect, but with our balanced approach, we gather more tools for our toolbox and have more skills of protection that we can call upon.

GROUNDING

Earth is the path of practicality. Earth is the path of roots. When we are harmed by others, we are usually not grounded in our foundations. The foundation of our body, our own truth and our personal power, is the soil where our roots grow. If we are not in touch with our authentic self, it is easy to be disturbed or knocked off balance, physically, emotionally, mentally, and spiritually. When we are centered, we are aware. We are not easily disturbed, and when we are, we easily find our footing again.

Grounding is a state of being. When we are ungrounded, energetically we are not fully present in our body or surroundings. A part of us has left. When we are in shock, from an accident or trauma, a part of our energy detaches from the body. Usually it comes back and becomes integrated as we come out of shock. Sometimes it leaves completely, causing what shamans call "soul loss" and a situation in need of deeper healing. When our energy is more anchored to the body and the world, such situations are not as likely to occur. I use flower essences, energetic remedies, to help reintegrate in cases of shock or high stress. Commercial brands readily available for such situations are Bach's Rescue Remedy and FES Five Flower Formula. These remedies energetically encourage the energy bodies to integrate with the physical body. They prevent long-term effects of shock.

Some people come into the world with a greater sense of grounding. These are the practical, sensible, down-to-earth types we all know. Then there are others who find that the physical world is usually a challenge, and never remain here too long when their mind could be wandering instead. These are the flighty, airy, and what is often labeled the "New Agey" people of our communities. They just have a different perception and reaction to the world and are not always fully present physically. Other people fall somewhere between the two extremes. Even if you have great natural grounding tendencies, it helps to learn how to evoke this energy on purpose, whenever it is needed.

GROUNDING TECHNIQUES

Grounding can be more difficult to do than you think. When meditating, doing shamanic journey or ritual, or even facing the stressful rigors of daily life, we encounter forces that throw us off balance. You can become ungrounded if someone or something shocks you. If you take on too much energy, even if it is "good" energy, you can become unbalanced and ungrounded. If you are too focused on the energetic and spiritual realms, even when your visionary experience is over, you are ungrounded. If your mind is simply wandering and you feel spacey and can't bring yourself back even when you need to be present, you are ungrounded. But the cure may be easier to find than you think. Here are some grounding techniques that will bring you back to your roots.

Body Awareness

Bringing your awareness to your body is very powerful. Stretching or performing other gentle movements where you pay attention to muscle sensations brings you back into your body. Even more vigorous forms of exercise, when done in a mindful way, can facilitate this process.

Earthing

One of the easiest ways to ground is to actually make contact with the ground. At the end of many rituals and meditations, practitioners are aided by either pressing their feet, often barefoot, on the ground. Others get on their hands and knees and press into their palms, imagining the unwanted energy flowing out of the crown and hands and into the earth. The energy is returned to the Earth. If you can't get on the ground, you can direct the energy into the ground through your hands, through an altar, or through a staff, sword, or other medium that conducts magickal energy.

Any "negative" or harmful energies will not hurt the Earth when doing this technique. Like a leaf, root, or body returned to the land, the Earth will break it down and turn it back into a more usable form. You can return it to the Earth with the intention that it be used for the healing and balancing of the Earth. One of my students, Karen, describes harmful energy like fertilizer. What may become poison in your body can be great for your garden.

Tree Hugging

Although this technique is associated with the generation of free love, it is quite metaphysically sound. Just like earthing, you are using an energy-conducting medium to make a connection to the earth and feel a sense of rootedness. I remember being in a meditation workshop where, during the break, people went out to hug trees. I thought they were crazy, but they encouraged me to do it, and it worked. It makes sense when you think of it metaphysically.

In this technique, you are making an exchange with the tree spirit itself, and as you give it some energy, you receive its grounded yet open energy. Ideally, you should use your intuition to make sure the tree wants a hug. I've met quite a few trees that didn't want me to assume they were willing magickal partners. I needed my manners and had to ask.

Growing Roots

Imagine yourself as a great tree with roots growing from either your legs and feet or, if sitting cross-legged, from the base of your spine, your root chakra. Feel your roots sink through the building you may be in, and into the soil. Feel the roots dig deeper through the Earth's crust, going unharmed into the mantle and ultimately deep enough to touch the core, and feel the beat of Mother Earth's heart.

If you don't feel grounded with this visualization, ask Mother Earth for her grounding love, and feel your roots draw up earth energy, as if you were sucking through a straw. Feel the energy enter your body and fill your cells with denser, earthy energy. If you get "too much" energy, imagine the unneeded excess coming out of your crown and into the sky.

Sinking

Imagine yourself on a soft beach, and with each moment, your feet sink deeper into the sand, grounding you. You are firmly planted in the soil and centered in your power.

Grounding Cord

Bring your awareness to the spine. Feel your energy descending down the spine. In general, as energy rises, we open our awareness, but ascend out of the material. When our energy descends, it brings us more fully into the world. So intend your energy to flow down the spine and to the base of the spine at the root chakra. Imagine a beam of light projecting from the root down the body and into the Earth. Again, bring the beam down to the center of the Earth. With this grounding cord, you are like a balloon tied down to the world.

Try any of these techniques when you feel ungrounded. They can be used individually, or in any combination, depending on what works best for you.

BOUNDARY

The element of water rules the astral and emotional bodies. Through working with the power of water, we learn to draw boundaries and create a sense of personal space. Through work with our energy bodies, our aura, we learn to create a personal sacred space and create our own reality. People with a strong, healthy sense of self and space have a definite sense of presence when they enter the room. Those with a collapsed sense of self and space are more likely to get crowded. It works the same way emotionally, mentally, and spiritually. Those who don't have a strong sense of personal space and boundaries let other people walk all over them. Sometimes it is intentional, and sometimes it isn't, but the result can be the same. If you have a strong sense of boundaries, you make it clear, through your words, body language, and personal energy, that you are not to be taken advantage of.

When you don't have a strong sense of self and your boundaries, it is easy to get overwhelmed by the thoughts, emotions, and intentions of others, like literally being overrun by the waves of emotional energy others project. This is the nature of water. The floods of others will disrupt your gentle pool of water if you don't keep it safe from intrusion. Many people involved in magick are empathic, and easily pick up on the emotions of others but don't know how to stop the process. The lack of boundaries, the ability to identify excessively with others rather than your own sacred space, is the reason so many are overwhelmed by other people, both in daily life and during psychic work.

Boundaries come in all forms. Boundaries can involve speaking our truth and standing up for ourselves and our personal space or way of life. Sometimes the greatest act of protection is to simply tell someone you don't approve of their actions toward you and telling them to cease and desist. Boundaries can be about separating yourself from certain people, environments, or behavior. Making the separation detaches you from the unhealthy influence. Saying "no" can be the most powerful magickal word when it comes to magickal protection. I often think of self-defense classes where students are trained to escape a mugging or attack. One of the first techniques they learn is to yell "no." You might not have to yell "no" at a friend or co-worker as you would in a mugging, but you have to be firm and make clear boundaries when dealing with those who are close to you.

Other boundaries are more subtle. They are unspoken, but ever present. They represent the health of our psychic boundaries. When we draw our energetic boundaries, we stake a personal space and embody our sacred personal space. Most of the time our energetic boundary reflects our emotions, self-esteem, and personal awareness. People in the day-to-day world react to our psychic boundaries all the time, even though they are not consciously aware of it.

We interact with the auras of others, and such energetic exchanges give us subtle information about the other person, including their personal power, mood, and health. Such interactions remind me of the old tale of the two Japanese samurai confronting one another on a bridge. Honor demands that the less accomplished warrior step aside for the one with greater mastery. When two skilled warriors with a great energetic awareness meet, they make contact through their energy fields, assessing each other's strengths and weaknesses. From that interaction, they determine if one will step aside, or if a battle will prove superiority. Often no battle is needed, because all is demonstrated in the energy emitted by the warriors.

The spiritual warriors of Peru, shamans and spirit walkers, describe their energetic interactions, taking an energetic assessment of another in similar ways to the Japanese samurai. But these shamans add a step. If one bests the other, the "victor" is duty bound to teach the other how to attain the same level of skill. The skill is also dependent on spiritual awareness, so it isn't simply teaching one physical or psychic combat, but the path to enlightenment.

From that initial confrontation and merging of energy fields, a bond is formed to later transmit information. We make connections and exchanges with others all the time. We have such bonds with friends, family, co-workers, and lovers. In fact, when we have sex, our energy fields merge for a short time, transferring information from one to the other. After the energy fields are released and separated, they have been changed, continuing the process of growth and evolution.

Whenever we have an emotional exchange with someone, there is the potential to create such links across our boundaries. When we get mad, or someone gets mad at us, we create a link. I used to worry endlessly over not being liked. It didn't matter if twenty people in the room liked me; I would focus on the one person who didn't, and try to find out why. Not everyone will "click" and like each other in this lifetime. It's not personal. I got personal and emotional and created a link. I pressed their boundaries in an unhealthy way and crossed a line to create an unhealthy link. Now I have learned to live and let live. In reality, we have no boundaries—we are all linked. But in practicality, we must draw boundaries for our own health and well-being.

PROTECTION SHIELD TECHNIQUES

Few people know how to manipulate their aura—to consciously change and adapt their personal energetic boundaries—to create a change and increase their protection. This is the basic foundation of psychic protection. Through intent, one consciously connects to the auric energy and places an intention of protection and stability in it. The aura conforms to your thoughts and feelings. If you intend and feel your protective space, you will create it. The idea is not so much the idea of creating a shield to reflect energy, as it is creating strong boundaries, coupled with strong roots, to be centered in your own authentic power and sense of self.

Those who are in the public sphere must be particularly conscious of their protection shields. When you project your energy in public, you attract more attention and can be a greater target for unwanted energies, both consciously and unconsciously. Make sure you have your shield up if you work with the public in any interactive calling, such as in a large business or in social services, a healing profession, or the performing arts.

Public witches and pagan community leaders are particularly susceptible to judgments, misunderstandings, and unwanted energies. Because they are in a public arena with other magickal people, they are also more likely to confront someone with the actual knowledge and ability to perform a psychic attack or curse. Don't let this discourage you from being a public person. Instead, let it encourage you to be grounded and centered in your own sacred space and personal power.

Sealing Holes in Your Aura

The first thing to do when working with boundaries is to seal the holes you currently have energetically. Verbal and emotional exchanges that induce trauma literally traumatize our energy bodies, leaving holes, rips, and tears in the aura. If you visualize the aura as a ball or balloon of energy, imagine it with slow leaks and holes, where your vital energy is escaping, adding to your fatigue, stress, and lack of boundaries. With intent, you can seal these holes.

While in a meditative state, bring your attention to the space around your body, to the auric boundary that exists just beyond the length of your outstretched arms, and intuitively feel for holes. They often feel like patches of cold or currents of air flowing away from your body rather than around it. Imagine rolling a ball of white light like clay, and sealing the hole with it. The light will change to whatever color it needs to be to heal your aura. Repeat the process until you have sealed all the holes.

Crystal Sphere Protection Shield

While in a light meditative state, after you have sealed any holes in your aura, imagine the outer edge of the aura, at least the edge you perceive, crystallizing. Imagine yourself in a large crystal egg or sphere (figure 15). Some see it polished like a crystal ball, while others see it faceted like a diamond. It is translucent, allowing energies you need to pass into it, but reflecting and neutralizing harmful, unwanted energies. I avoid visualizing it as strict white light, since white light is so protective that it can block out all energies, even energy you desire to attract. I state the following information when doing my shield meditation:

"I charge this protection shield to protect me from all harmful energies, both positive and negative.

I charge this protection shield to protect me from all harmful energies, both positive, negative, and otherwise.

I charge this protection shield to protect me from all harm, and reflect love back on the source of the harm.

I charge this shield to protect me from all physical harm, from all physical and energetic pollution, attacks, and harmful intentions, both of my own making and from others. So mote it be."

You should reaffirm this protection shield regularly as a part of your meditative practice.

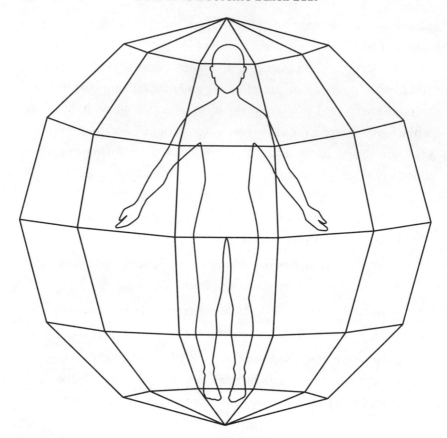

Figure 15: Crystal Sphere Protection Shield

Projecting a Shield

You can "crystallize" the energy fields around not only yourself, but also your home, car, children, pets, and anything else. You shouldn't be throwing such shields around people unless you have their permission, but if I am a passenger in someone else's car, I will put a protection shield around the entire car with the intention that if it is not for the highest good, it will fade when our journey together is over. Shields will fade in time. If you need a permanent shield, you will have to reinforce it periodically.

Circling Rings

Another way of creating a protective space is to trace a circle around your body, home, or anything else. Visualize a ring of multicolored, prismatic light coming from your fingertip, wand, or athame, and then trace your circle with it. This is usually done with your power hand, or dominant hand, but in a pinch, either hand will work. Traditionally, do this three times. You are not casting a full circle, but creating a space that will move as you move. Many see the three rings move independently and rotating in different directions, creating the image of a sphere.

Sacred Geometry

Since a multitude of symbols and shapes are known for their protective powers, the power of sacred geometry comes in many forms. You can visualize the protection symbols from chapter 4. Hold the image in your mind and project it outward, in front of you or behind you, or wherever you feel the potential for harm. I prefer to visualize or draw a pentagram. The banishing pentagram, used in many traditions to ward off all harm on any level, is drawn by starting at the bottom-left point, as you are looking at it, and moving to the top, until you complete the five strokes of the star. Almost daily, I draw the pentagram in every direction, including above and below, along with the circling rings, to create a protective shield.

The last form of sacred-geometry protection is to visualize the shapes of sacred geometry, particularly the Platonic solids, around you, much like the crystal sphere protection shield. I often visualize a pyramid-like structure around my home, like the top half of an octahedron. Or I visualize the entire octahedron, with half above the ground and half below it (figure 16).

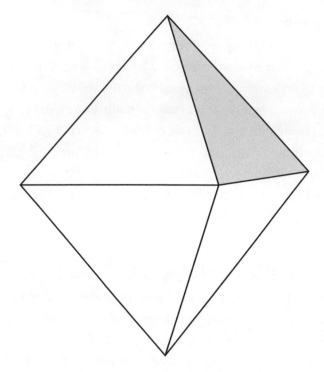

Figure 16: Octahedron

Mirrors

I have read a lot about this particular technique, but do not recommend it. It involves visualizing yourself surrounded by mirrors or a mirror-like coating that reflects all harm back to the sender. Many witches use this technique quite effectively, but I have issues with the ethics involved. I don't believe it is our place to return the energy to the sender. You may feel it is justified, but the Wiccan Rede states: "And it harm none, do what you will." Harm none being the operative phrase. It doesn't say: "An eye for an eye." Such witches equate it with the Law of Three, ever popular in modern witchcraft, which says that what they send out must be returned to them threefold. This return effect is the principle of magick.

Everything eventually returns, wanted or unwanted, to its source. The universe magnifies the energy to manifest it as a physical reality. But it is not your job to determine when, where, and how it will be returned. I find it akin to being shot at and having the ability to reflect the bullet back at the shooter. Yes, you are defending yourself, but what if someone else is caught in the crossfire? If you have the ability to return it, you also have the ability to ground it and make sure that it hurts no one. You can take appropriate measures to guarantee your protection, but it is not your job to punish the guilty. The "karma police" are not taking applications, so simply live your own life as morally as you can and harm none. You will be taken care of in return.

MENTAL FLEXIBILITY

Mental flexibility is a true key to protection and problem solving. Often, energies and issues are only a problem and only cause us harm when we make them into problems. The way we react to and process difficult situations and people is half the battle. We put so much energy into the struggle that we get sucked into the drama of the situation. The more energy and attention we give it, the larger the problem can become, until it seems insurmountable.

If we choose to frame the situation differently, we can transmute the energy and have a completely different experience. If we label it differently, we transform a problem or curse into a great lesson. Many of my most difficult experiences have been my greatest teachers. Many of the worst people in my life, personally, professionally, and in and out of the craft, have been my wisest teachers. Perhaps they didn't realize they were teaching me something. They often taught me more about how I don't want to be and how to draw appropriate boundaries, but they were great life-changing teachers.

When we frame trauma, conflict, illness, injury, and even psychic attack as potential teachers, suddenly the process takes a new focus in our mind. We no longer put our energy into fighting against something, but rather learning from it, with the thought in mind that once we learn from the experience, we will detach from it completely. Once it serves its purpose, we will release it and be that much stronger for having experienced it.

Witches must also be vigilant in their thought processes. We create our own reality, and our thoughts, words, and deeds often attract the experiences in our life. We are often unconscious of our words and say things we don't truly mean, but as we grow in magickal power, we realize that all our words and thoughts have power. Something we say in jest or in a moment of confusion can help create our reality. And our thoughts can contribute to unintentional psychic attack, or at least bombardment, of others.

When we put ourselves or others down, or unfairly judge, gossip, or speak in anger, we create energy and project it. In chapter 1, we discussed how our harmful judgments, projections, and insults make the recipient weaker physically. It lowers both physical and psychic strength, and decreases the power of the immune, nervous, and glandular systems. But our insults and unhealthy thoughts do return to us eventually. Often we are our own worst enemies when it comes to psychic protection.

Neutralization

One technique I learned from one of my first teachers, Laurie Cabot, and later found that many other mystical traditions use, is neutralization. All thought is energy, and once something is thought, it is sent out into the universe. It cannot be called back. Energy cannot be created or destroyed, but simply transformed. Neutralization is taking responsibility for the thought, but creating another thought to ground and transform the original unwanted thought. If I say something that I do not want to manifest, I immediately follow those words with "I neutralize that." If I visualize something unwanted, often through my own fears, I visualize a white X through the image, neutralizing it. When I first learned magick, I was not conscious of my thoughts, and said many insults and comments in poor taste. I was saying "I neutralize that" over and over again for many moons.

DIRECT ACTION

Direct action is one of my last resorts when it comes to psychic self-defense. Most of the other techniques are more preventative in nature. Action refers to a proactive technique, usually called curse breaking or hex breaking. This is the stance of the spiritual warrior, one who defends the truth and prevents harm by taking action. The harmful, unwanted energy is identified and neutralized. Steps are taken to ensure future safety through spells of binding. Most often, if you get to this stage, it is because there is someone who intends you harm. The person may or may not be a magickal practitioner, but will have a strong, fiery will and the energy to put it to use.

These warrior techniques help you assess the situation and take steps to prevent further harm. They are some of the most powerful forms of protection magick, but are needed infrequently if you practice the other forms of magickal protection in the previous sections.

Triangle of Defense

The Triangle of Defense technique comes from the arts of high magick, and is a very effective method of recognizing and neutralizing a harmful psychic attack from any source. I originally learned it from avid fans of *Modern Magick* by Donald Michael Kraig, but it can also be found in Denning and Phillips' *Practical Guide to Psychic Self-Defense and Well-Being.*

Start by closing your eyes and turning slowly in a clockwise circle with the intention of feeling the direction from which a psychic attack is originating. I usually feel it like a buzzing in my third eye. Others feel it in their hands, heart, or solar plexus. Once you find it, stand your ground and face it like a warrior. Visualize a pentagram in cobalt-blue or violet light at your third eye. Bring your hands up to your third eye, palms facing out, thumbs touching together, and first fingers touching together, creating a triangle at the forehead. This motion is usually called the Triangle of Manifestation and is used in spell work to consecrate tools and charms. Here, it is manifesting your will for protection.

Step forward (tradition says with your left foot, but I step forward with my right) and project your hands forward, sending the triangle to the source of harm, severing the link and shielding you from future harm. Ceremonial magicians would seal this process with the Lesser Banishing Ritual of the Pentagram, or LBRP, found in chapter 7, to prevent future attack. For now, you can simply do a cleansing and banishing ritual with banishing pentagrams in all directions, smudge, or use any other technique that suits you.

Advanced Psychic Defense

Although some traditions follow more formal protocols of defense techniques akin to a martial-art series of moves, I have learned and created an eclectic toolbox of defense techniques. All of them require a strong awareness and will and the ability to be creative, and often involve complex visualizations. Like the Triangle of Defense technique, they use ritualistic movements, visualizations, and intent.

If you sense any type of energetic attack, mentally create an energetic shield to block the attack from whatever direction you feel is vulnerable. Imagine literally a square, rectangle, or circle of energy acting like a knight's shield to protect you.

Imagine gaining control of harmful energy directed toward you, like waves or lines of light. Take the lines and weave them together, and visualize them knotted, much like a tangled Celtic knot, and then place it in the ground. This is particularly powerful when facing psychic attack from nonphysical entities.

Once I felt that a particularly empathic acquaintance was purposely intruding on my mental space, trying to read my mood and mind. It felt like a hook digging into my brow. Intuitively, I visualized two Arabian swords, or scimitars, above my head, crossing at the brow, severing the link and moving down my chakra column, breaking all harmful connections to my energy system (figure 17).

Figure 17: Scimitars

By combining a bit of sympathetic ritual magick and psychic self-defense, you can create a false target. You can visualize yourself separating from a created image of yourself. Imagine yourself literally stepping out of your body, leaving an "after-image" in your wake that will be the target of harm. Imagine a sword between you, or ritualistically use your athame, your ritual blade, to cut your link to this mirror image. Then place the image in a poppet, magickal doll, stuffed animal, box, pillow, or anything else. I would fill the poppet, or whatever container you use, with protective herbs. Others might fill it with sea salt. Herbs and salt will neutralize any harm. In any case, the most important step is to remove it from your home and bury it somewhere at least a few miles away. That will be the target of harm, continually grounding and neutralizing harm directed toward you, acting as a sacrificial lamb.

Be creative in your defensive techniques, keeping in mind the Law of Three and the Wiccan Rede.

Spell Craft

Will is the tool of the fiery warrior and the first component to any true spell craft. Spell craft involves more complicated preventative measures, such as wards, protection potions, and amulets, as well as the complex art of hex breaking, where specific harmful energies are identified and removed. Though archaic magick books will say the best defense to a curse is to curse the curser, I highly disagree with this. Never do your own curses to protect yourself or to seek revenge. They will only harm you in the end by returning to you even more magnified. If someone is actually doing curses against you, they will reap the consequences of their own actions soon enough. Focus on breaking this harmful link by understanding what lesson the situation is bringing you. By understanding the lesson, you can integrate its message and prevent many future harmful situations. Protective spell craft will be discussed in detail in chapter 7.

SPIRIT

The defensive techniques of spirit are the ones people turn to the least, but these techniques are the most important and should be foremost in your mind when taking any other defensive measure. All the elements spring from the element of spirit, and all the elements also return to spirit. Through the power of spirit, a witch realizes that all things are connected. We are all part of the Great Spirit, the divine mind. We are all like cells within the body of the Goddess. When we wage conflict, we are one body, divided from within. I am reminded of the Native American saying "It is a foolish tree whose branches fight amongst themselves." What tree could survive in such an absurd way? Then how can the human family tree, or greater still, the Earth tree, with all animals and plants, survive in a constant state of conflict?

Fear is the source of this conflict. Hate is not the opposite of love. Hate and love are quite close in nature. Fear is the polarity of love. Fear allows us to see others as so completely different from ourselves that we can make a complete division. When you know magick, you know the truth: there is no division. Everything is connected.

One of the reasons witches do magick as part of their spiritual path is to truly know that everything is connected. When you do a spell for a job and you run into someone randomly who gives you information about the job, you are recognizing your connection to that person through the spirit of the Goddess and God. You were always connected and always will be connected, but in that moment, you sent your intention and the universe filled it by making you aware of the connection that is ever present. My friend Alixaendreia always reminds herself in any conflict that her "opponent" is "simply another me." Each has the same spirit running through the body, but with a different point of view. The Hindu traditions say that we live in the Maya, the illusion of the world that creates separation, while the truth is that we are all one. We have difficulty seeing this when we are in the illusion.

The true path of the spiritual warrior is the way of compassion. Compassion is found at the true heart of all spiritual paths. In Wicca, we call it Perfect Love and Perfect Trust. Compassion starts with yourself, and then compassion for others you know. If you can hold compassion for yourself, then you can truly hold it for a stranger and ultimately for those who seek to harm you.

COMPASSIONATE DEFENSE

How can defense be compassionate? By recognizing that there is no "other." When you send harmful energy away, realize that there is no "away." When you sever an unhealthy connection, you are still connected. We are all one in our uniqueness and diversity. Instead of severing, cutting away, isolating, or blocking the experience, seek to heal it. If we are cells in the body of the universe, when we fight, it's like cancer in the body, cells fighting cells. Our ego tells us that we are the valiant immune system, fighting the evil "cancer" cells of our enemies. This happens most often in times of war. It is easy to label the enemy as evil, but when we rise above the ego, we often realize that things are not as cut and dried as simple good and evil. When both are working from the ego point of view, and not the higher reality, it is easy to miss the complexity of any situation.

In the body, illness occurs when there is dis-ease, stress, tension, or blocked energy, when that part of the body comes out of alignment with the greater whole. True holistic healing comes about when the offending parts of the body are not removed, but brought back into balance. We come from a society that is quick to cut things out rather than soothe, heal, and nurse them back to health. We treat our enemies the same way, rather than understanding why we are out of alignment and performing supportive acts to bring us both back into harmony.

Although in previous chapters I've associated compassion with water, as it is an emotion, on the highest level it is the most spiritual response we can have to a situation, moving beyond the emotional realm to the highest realm of spirit.

Reflection

Before you take any action, reflect on your situation. Meditate, and ask to see the higher purpose of this conflict in your life. Regardless of whether the conflict is with a person, entity, or community, reflect. True spiritual reflection takes introspection to the next level. Is the difficulty teaching you something? Is it pushing your buttons, your weak spots? Are you teaching others something? When there is teaching, it is usually on both sides simultaneously. Does this feel like a test of your integrity or spirituality? If so, how are you faring? Are you reacting, or hopefully acting and not reacting, in the way you would envision to be the highest and best course? If not, why not?

Before you banish a situation completely, ask to understand it. If it has a purpose, but you dismiss it, new situations with similar themes will occur over and over again until you acknowledge them and learn from them. Then you can move forward.

Blessing

"Bless your enemies away" is the advice of Luisa Teish, from her tape series *Jumbalaya,* based on the book of the same name. When someone is attacking you or making your life miserable, intentionally or unintentionally, they are usually not happy in their own life, and are using you as a distraction or scapegoat for their own unhappiness. If you send them blessings rather than curses, they become occupied with their good fortune, taking their attention off of you. Wish them health, wealth, and prosperity. Wish them the fulfillment of their desires, for the highest good. Wish them well as you wish them away from your life. You are sending out blessings and will receive only blessings back, since you are doing no harm to anyone.

This is the magickal equivalent of "killing them with kindness," though I dislike that phrase. You are not being phony or manipulative, but genuinely a vessel for divinity. I had a teacher who suggested that when all else fails and you don't know what to do, or you don't know what you are supposed to learn from a situation or person, simply be open to your antagonist. Remain as detached and loving toward the person as you can. In meditation, imagine the person surrounded with loving light, for the highest good. You are not visualizing specific behavior or controlling their will. This teacher felt that gold-colored light was the best, the highest divine love. You don't have to love or bless the person personally, but try to approach the situation from a place of divinity. If you are open to the person, they might be open to you or, at the very least, detach from the situation and leave you alone.

Laughter

Laughter is the best defense. If you don't take something seriously, you often diffuse it. Laughter works for magickal attacks, psychic entities, and good old-fashioned quarrels. My friend Christopher Giroux, a tarot counselor, was once asked by a client how to defeat black magick by evil witches. His reply was to laugh it off. It works, and it's the simplest thing to do. It seems too simple, and some who consider themselves serious practitioners ignore this advice because they believe that to do magick, you must do something complicated; but laughter has very sound magickal principles behind it.

When you take a situation very seriously, you often contract your energy in defense. Though a temporary help, through fear you often stay in a more contracted energetic space and cannot express your full power or be as open to your intuition. Fear contracts and can even lead to energetic blocks and illness. Also, when you are in fear, but put a lot of thought and energy into an unhealthy relationship, you create a circuit of energy between the two of you. You create an unhealthy cord where you are able to energetically "pull" or "rattle" each other's "chain." You become more reactive. Your intensity can add energy to the spell or entity that is plaguing you. The more you fight it, and get hooked into the fight, the conflict, the polarization of "me versus them," the more fuel you add to the fire.

Only when you energetically disengage and detach from the situation emotionally and mentally do you cut the fire off from its source. Most entities who are fearsome feed off your fear. They have little energy themselves, so they play-act to seem like they are big monsters to scare psychically sensitive people. The more fear you feed them, the stronger the manifestation. If you laugh at them, you cut their food supply and render them impotent. You see them for what they are and deem them beneath your notice. Without your attention, they no longer get what they are seeking and leave, or are easily banished, lacking the energy to resist.

When you laugh off attacks from people, magickal or otherwise, you are diffusing the situation with humor. A family squabble can often be laughed off together, but in the case of "evil" witches or magicians, nothing frustrates them more than to not be taken seriously. They are doing such acts for attention, because they feel they are powerful. When you laugh at their act of power, you are breaking the circuit, and they will seek new power trips with those who will play into their games.

Ultimately, laughter that comes from the heart is laughter of love, of joy. When you laugh from the heart, you are neutralizing any harmful energy with love, the most powerful magick possible. At the same time, you are sending out love, so if it returns to you threefold, you are triply blessed.

CHAPTER 6

SOMEBODY'S WATCHING ME

Angels, deceased relatives, and totem animals are all spirits ascribed the power of protection by various spiritual traditions. The concept of protective spirits reaches back to the dawn of civilization and continues to play an important role today in both indigenous cultures and industrial nations. Not only do we feel the need for protection and guidance, but we find a sense of guardianship from those not in this physical world. In my work, I come across many people with no involvement in the occult who feel they have a guardian angel or, even more common, a passed love one who watches over them and guides them out of danger.

EVOCATION

Many of the most primal forms of magick are for contacting or summoning spirits of protection for an individual, for a home, and often for a tomb or ancestral land. Rituals, vision quests, and prayers are all forms of magick to connect with protective spirits. Once a link is established, a relationship can be built with these spirits. Some spirits take on many functions, acting as guide or a healer as well as a protector. Others are simply called to provide protection. Known as *gatekeepers,* such spirits can psychically guard gateways in the world, or the gateways of consciousness, into your soul.

One common factor in mystical traditions is the concept of evocation. To really receive the benefit of these protective spirits, they must be actively invited into life. Though many spirits will protect instinctually and intuitively for your higher good, most will not directly contact you or get involved until you invite them into your life because they don't want to violate your free will. Evocation is the magickal act of summoning a spirit.

Evocation rituals in traditional magick are often complicated. They can involve reciting special words of power, usually involving the name of the spirit, or drawing a symbol of the spirit, or holding a talisman of material associated with the spirit.

In my practice, I like to contact spirits via meditation. Once I have made contact with the spirit, I feel we can commune outside of meditation. I can sense the spirit's presence in my daily life. When I call upon that spirit for guidance or protection, I feel that through my previous connection with it, I have its spiritual "phone number" or "hotline," so to speak, and can put a direct call in for immediate assistance. Here is a simple evocation I teach students who seek protective spirits:

> *"I, (state your name), now call upon my highest guardian spirits to protect me from all harm. Hail and welcome."*

The process is so simple, yet so effective. Usually, you will feel the presence of your guardian spirits. Even if you don't, particularly if you are in a highly stressful situation, know that these protective spirits are there for you.

If you have meditated with a specific spirit and know its name, or it has given you a symbol, you can call the spirit by name or visualize its symbol. Let your intuition guide you. A symbol of evocation, for any type of spirit or gateway, is the basic evocation pentagram (figure 18).

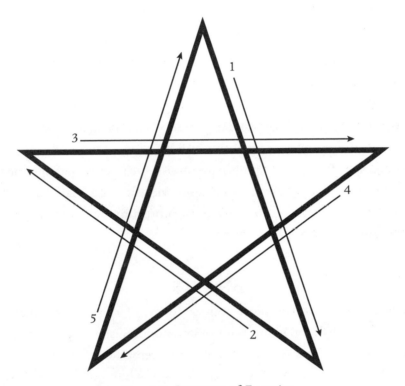

Figure 18: Pentagram of Evocation

Used like a key, this gesture opens up a gateway or evokes a spirit when used with your intention. To release or close it, use the banishing pentagram with the intention of closing the spirit connection.

After the spirit is called, in your mind or out loud, tell it what you fear. Ask for specific protection from such threats. If I'm walking home and feel unsafe, or see an erratic driver on the highway near me, or fear the strong psychic emanations of very unhappy people around me, I evoke my protection spirit. I also back it up with other protection techniques, such as the psychic protection shield.

When in doubt as to which spirit you want to call, this basic prayer of protection evokes the Goddess, God, and Great Spirit:

> *"I, (state your name), call upon the Goddess, God, and Great Spirit to protect me from all harm."*

You can start and end your day with a protective spirit evocation. I make it a part of my morning meditations, asking for protection throughout the day. At the end of my day, I ask my guardians to protect my body while I sleep and my spirit while I travel in my dreams.

This simple type of evocation can be used in all situations, although specific types of spirits have specific techniques and offerings for protection. The rest of this chapter includes information about different spirits that can be evoked for protection, including angels, power animals, and pagan deities.

ANGELS

Angels are one of the most popular forms of spiritual guardians. Since they are found in the mainstream monotheistic religions, most people are not afraid of angels and don't even think of them as spirits. Due to their Biblical associations, pagans often dislike working with them, feeling they are too Christian. I know I felt that way initially. Angels have a rich history, and such beings are found in many magickal cultures. In such mythologies, angels are not the familiar winged cherubs found on greeting cards, but powerful beings with a variety of forms. The blessings of the angelic realm belong to every culture.

Angelic lore is very complex and comes from a variety of conflicting sources. In the end, I believe you should have your own experience with the angels and go by the messages and techniques they give you. Angels are often divided into a hierarchy of groups called *choirs*. Some angels deal directly with humanity, while others have functions in the universe that make them more distant and remote from humanity.

Although we use the term *angel* as a catch-all phrase for these beings, technically it belongs to the choir of angels most commonly associated with humanity. They act as companion spirits, guides, and protectors, and seem the most human in our direct experience. Here we find the popular concept of guardian angels. Everyone is said to have a guardian angel for protection. This spirit can protect the physical body as well as the spiritual selves. You can use an evocation to call upon your guardian angel, as described in the previous section.

In certain forms of ceremonial magick, the *Holy Guardian Angel* is a term for the higher self of the magician. All works of high magick bring one closer to "Knowledge and Conversation of the Holy Guardian Angel." This simply means that magick is used for spiritual evolution, to meet and begin a relationship with your higher divine self, and ultimately to learn to embody more and more of it in your daily life.

Out of all the many choirs of angels, the archangels are better known by the general public. There names are found in the myths of the three major monotheistic religions, Judaism, Christianity, and Islam. They are the messengers of God to humanity. I prefer to think of them as messengers and embodiments of the great creative spirit, not just the God of the Bible. Although there are many archangels, the most popular ones found in Western magick are those who are guardians of the four directions.

Raphael: Raphael is the guardian of the east and the element of air. Known as the physician of the angelic realm, Raphael can be called upon for healing work. Art depicts Raphael with a wand, or caduceus, or sometimes a sword. Raphael's colors are yellow and violet.

Michael: Michael is the guardian of the south and the element of fire. As keeper of the flaming sword, Michael is the most powerful angelic archetype for the spiritual warrior. Some images depict him with a spear instead of a sword. Michael's colors are red and green. I call upon Michael all the time for protection from anything from unwanted spirits in my healing work to reckless drivers on the highway.

Gabriel: Gabriel is the guardian of the west and the element of water. This archangel is the messenger with a magickal trumpet. Gabriel is also associated with the chalice or Holy Grail. Gabriel's colors are blue and orange.

Uriel: Uriel is the guardian of the north and the element of earth. This archangel is often the favorite of pagans and witches. Uriel is also associated with Mother Earth, and death in the sense of returning the body to the earth. His tool is the stone or pentacle. Uriel's usual color associations are earth tones, such as green, brown, and black, though some magicians associate black and silver with this archangel.

Pillar of Light

One of the first angelic rituals I learned was from the founder of Shamballa Reiki, John Artimage. Through his channeled material working with the angelic realm, he suggested an exercise calling upon Archangel Michael. It was so simple that I thought it couldn't possibly be that easy to access the aid of the angelic realm. But when I used it, I truly felt an angelic presence.

This technique involves a pillar of light, much like the Middle Pillar of Qabalistic ceremonial magick, going around and through the body of the practitioner. It starts in the source of creation, visualized as some cosmic center, and descends down around you, through the ground, and anchors in the heart of the Earth. It blocks out any un-wanted forces that are attacking you, consciously or unconsciously. Only things that "belong" to you remain in the pillar. So if you are feeling overwhelmed by other people and their feelings and psychic projections, create this pillar. If you still feel this way, then it's not other people you need to deal with, but your own emotions.

Unlike the Qabalistic Middle Pillar, this beam can last indefinitely and it moves as you move. You don't have to do any heavy visualization or chanting. You can do it in your car, office, or home without much notice. To activate it, simply say, silently in your mind or out loud: "Archangel Michael, give me a pillar of light to protect me from all harm." Then feel the pillar descend around you. It might be very strong or very subtle, but it is there. In my experience, it can last for an hour or up to a day, but it needs to be renewed periodically. I use this technique when I feel the need for immediate protection, and use my other psychic defense methods for continual protection.

Cutting Psychic Cords with Archangel Michael

Another powerful technique I learned from Shamballa Reiki is call-ing upon Archangel Michael to cut all inappropriate psychic cords and links with others. When we get into an unhealthy emotional ex-change with others, we have the potential to create a psychic link with them, until those emotions are resolved. Some think of such ex-changes as the building blocks of karma. Through this meditation, you can release and heal those ties that are longstanding, and with regular use, prevent the creation of new unhealthy cords.

While in a meditative state, simply call upon Archangel Michael and ask him to cut with his flaming sword all unhealthy ties that do not serve your highest good. Go through all sides of your body and aura. Ask Michael to cut the cords down your front, down your back, to your left and to your right, above and below. Ask Michael to cut all inappropriate cords from all seven chakras, starting at the root and going upward. When done, thank Archangel Michael. Then you can go on to the healing technique described in the next section.

For an alternate form of energetic cord cutting and aura healing, see chapter 11 in my book *The Inner Temple of Witchcraft: Magick, Meditation and Psychic Development*.

Angelic Healing

After any type of psychic exchange that feels like an attack, when you are ill, or just when you are in need of a spiritual tune-up, you can call upon the angelic realm to help you. Sometimes prevention and maintenance are the most appropriate defenses.

While in a meditative state, call upon Archangel Raphael, the healer, to help you. Feel his energy envelop you in a ball of light. The light can be any color that is appropriate for you. After the light co-coon wraps itself around you, anything can happen, and it will be different in each healing session. Everyone will feel, hear, and see things differently. The angels under Raphael may guide you to different positions or give you messages. You could go into a deep sleep until the healing is done. You might not feel anything, but it is still working.

Stay in the healing field as long as you feel you need to be there. The minimum I've used is about ten minutes, and the longest around two hours. When done, thank Raphael and return from your meditative state by grounding yourself in the physical world.

Lesser Banishing Ritual of the Pentagram

Another Qabalistic technique popular in other disciplines, including modern witchcraft, is the Lesser Banishing Ritual of the Pentagram, also known as the LBRP for short. It is a cleansing, clearing, and protective ritual done daily by certain magicians to create protection and vitality, and to call upon the four archangels of the quarters for continual support during the day. It "grounds" the Qabalistic Tree-of-Life structure in your energy body.

The LBRP involves ritual movements and chanting words of power in Hebrew, which later became the basis of the Lord's Prayer. Though many witches might find this displeasing, I urge you to try it and see how the energy feels. I find this ceremony very powerful, and Hebrew is a very magickal language. Witches who like the ceremony but dislike the Hebrew associations, change the language or make variations of the ritual. I've done similar rituals, but called upon the Celtic goddesses and gods for the four directions rather than the angels, because I feel a greater kinship with them. But the angelic ritual is very powerful.

The LBRP consists of four parts. It begins with the Qabalistic Cross ritual, the second part is the actual banishment ritual, the third part is the evocation of the four archangels, and the ending is a repetition of the Qabalistic Cross ritual.

QABALISTIC CROSS

Face east and take a few deep breaths. Stand firm and tall.
Point to your forehead with your right hand or with your blade.
Visualize a beam of white light entering your crown chakra.
Imagine your crown is the top of the Tree of Life (figure 19).

Chant: **Ata**

Point to the root chakra or the ground with your right hand.
Visualize the beam of light descending from the crown, down to the
root, then down to the earth between your feet.
Imagine the bottom sphere of the Tree of Life between your feet.
Feel a connection between the crown and the earth.

Chant: **Malkuth**

Point to your right shoulder with your right hand.
Visualize a beam of light from the space to your right that comes
into the right shoulder.

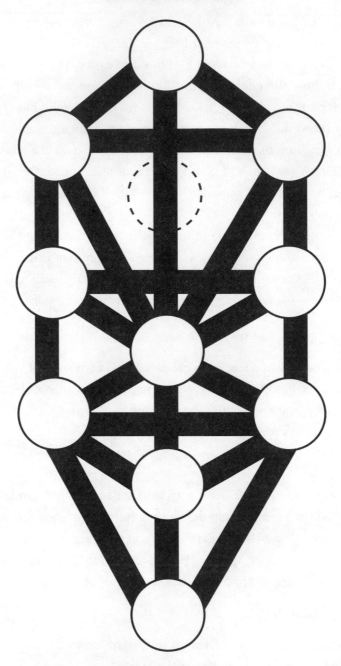

Figure 19: Tree of Life

Chant: **Veh Gebura**

Point to your left shoulder with your right hand.

Visualize the beam of light moving across from the right shoulder to the left shoulder, crossing the first vertical beam at the heart/throat area. Feel the beam of light move out of the left shoulder and out into the space to your left.

Chant: **Veh Gadula**

Bring your hands to your heart center in prayer position, palms pressed together.

Chant: **Le Oh Lam**

Focus on the cross in the middle of your body. Feel your self grounded and balanced.

Chant: **Amen**

Focus on your connection to all.

Banishing Ritual

Face east.

Draw a banishing pentagram in blue light.

Chant: **Yud Heh Vahv Heh**

Turn clockwise, drawing one quarter of a circle in light.
Face south.
Draw a banishing pentagram in blue light.

Chant: **Adonai**

Turn clockwise, drawing one quarter of a circle in light.
Face west.
Draw a banishing pentagram in blue light.

Chant: **Eh Heh Eh**

Turn clockwise, drawing one quarter of a circle in light.
Face north.
Draw a banishing pentagram in blue light.

Chant: **Agla**

Turn clockwise, drawing one quarter of a circle in light to complete
the circle.
Face east again.

EVOCATION OF THE ARCHANGELS

Chant: **Before me Raphael**
　　　Behind me Gabriel
　　　On my right hand Michael
　　　On my left hand Uriel
　　　Before me shines the pentagram

Stretch out your arms and legs and visualize yourself as a banishing
pentagram.

Chant: **Within me shines the six-rayed star**

Visualize a hexagram, a six-pointed star, in your heart chakra.
Repeat the Qabalistic Cross.

There are more formal and complicated versions of the LBRP found
in the traditions of ceremonial magick. They involve specific ritual
movements and gestures to empower each pentagram, but this is the
first and simplest version I learned, and similar versions are often
practiced by witches. It is a great way to start using ceremonial magick in your practice.

　　Authors trying to convey the power in the sound of magickal
words, particularly in rituals like the LBRP, go into such detail about

the proper formula for toning the words of the ritual that beginners start out terribly frightened that they are doing it wrong, so they opt not to try it at all. Instructions vary from tradition to tradition. Some tone the words higher than the speaking voice, and others lower. Many hold particular syllables for a set amount of time. I've heard many version of the LBRP and they all seemed to work for the practitioner. I urge you to simply try it and find what works for you.

Although in conversation and meditations I refer to the archangels in a casual way, with the more modern pronunciations, their names are more formal in the toning of the LBRP. The three syllables are emphasized in the toning of the names. Michael is chanted "Mik-i-el." If you prefer, you can use the more casual pronunciations in your own execution of the LBRP. Use what is most effective for you.

These are just a few of the powerful techniques of angelic magick. You could also do a magick circle ritual (see chapter 7) and call upon the four archangels for protection. Build your relationship with the angels and see what gifts they bring you.

POWER ANIMALS

Animal spirits are powerful protective allies. In South American traditions, along with most other shamanic cultures, the animal ally is said to be a great protector, shielding us from evil spirits, illness, and accident. One who dies young was said to have offended his animal totem, who would then leave the young one unprotected. Through honoring and building your relationship with your totem, you gain a powerful ally. Much of shamanic healing involves either restoring previous relationships with offended animal spirits, or finding a new animal spirit ally who will agree to protect and help.

All animal allies are protective in nature, regardless of what you think the animal would do in real life. Though a bear seems more protective than a butterfly, if your animal medicine is butterfly, then it will be protective for you. All animals are protective when in the spirit world. If it is your primary totem, then it is your spirit of protection. At the end of this section, I describe how to find your protective power animal through shamanic journey.

Here are some protective animal spirits you could actively evoke if you are not sure of your own animal spirit, or if you want additional help. Each one also carries other medicine, or wisdom, to help you live a life in balance.

Bear

Bear is a fierce warrior spirit, but it also holds the energy of introspection, urging us to go within regularly, like the bear's annual hibernation. The bear's size and power must be respected, but it also shows a side of gentleness and wisdom that all warriors need.

Owl

Owl is another protective spirit and is the symbol of the goddess Athena (see also the following section on protective deities). Owl helps protect us through wisdom, sometimes urging us not to be open about the power we hold, to only come out at night and remain invisible.

Skunk

Skunk protects by deterring its foes. Skunk also demands respect. Everyone knows the skunk and respects its power. Though its spray doesn't kill, it demonstrates a powerful, yet not lethal, show of power. Skunk medicine teaches self-confidence and self-acceptance.

Spider

Spider teaches us protection through fear. We learn to conquer primal fears with spider, and can take on a fearsome persona when needing to deter others. Spiders learn awareness and sensitivity, feeling the vibrations of all the strands as they sit in the center of their webs, waiting patiently. Spider webs on the spiritual planes are great shields of protection, netting harmful energy before it reaches us.

Stag

Stag teaches awareness through its mighty horn. Stag gods are fathers and forest masters, like Cernunnos. Witches call upon Cernunnos as a father protector god. Deer medicine, in general, can bring playfulness and softness, even in strength.

Turtle

Turtle medicine, with its hard shell and soft insides, is all about providing protection without turning hard toward those we need to be close to. In an effort to build psychic armor, we sometimes harden in all our relationships and lose our connection with the heart. Turtle is Mother Earth medicine, feeling the heart beat as we remain protected in the world.

Wolf

The first animal I learned to call upon was wolf. Witches often use wolf hair, or wolf-like dog hair, in protection potions. Wolves are clan animals and instill a sense of tight-knit family protection. If you are part of the wolf clan, you will be protected, even if wolf spirit is just temporarily adopting you. Wolf is also the medicine of the teacher. If you don't know your protective animal spirit, you can evoke the power of wolf to be with you.

Many more animals of protection exist. We each have our own favorite. Use this list as a starting place in your own animal mysteries.

Journeying to Find Your Protective Power Animal

You can do a shamanic journey to find your protective power animal. While listening to a drumming beat to induce a trance state, visualize a great tree, the shamanic World Tree, that connects you to the upper world and underworld of spirits. Look for a tunnel or opening in the tree and enter it with the beat of the drum. Imagine yourself going to the upper worlds or underworlds, looking for your animal. While in this trance, you will meet the spirit of your protective totem. The animal may make itself known to you directly, or you may see many animal spirits. Any animal that you see three times or more and that appears friendly to you, is probably your animal guide. Return the way you came, through the tunnel of the tree, and return to your body with the beat of the drum.

Once you know your protective animal, visit it often. Get a symbol, or fetish, to remind you of it, and carry it with you. Evoke your animal spirit in times of uncertainty, and thank it whenever you call upon it. These actions help develop your relationship with the animal spirit.

DEITIES OF PROTECTION

Many deities of the pagan world are patrons of protection for their followers. If you have a special relationship with any deity, regardless of their usual sphere of influence, you can call upon that god or goddess for protection. Because of your individual relationship, that deity will take special care of your well-being. Ideally, you should have a prior relationship with any deity you call upon for protection, but some gods are more attuned to be protectors. You may want to do meditations and rituals with them to build a relationship, particularly if you feel the need for their protection. They can be a part of your deeper spiritual work. At the end of this section, I describe how to find a god of protection through meditation.

The following deities are known in modern paganism for their power in the realm of protection. Most fit the archetype of divine parent, either mother or father, but some are gods of magick and travel, and others are warriors.

Ares/Mars

Although painted a villain in modern fictional lore, Ares is a god of war and warriors. Though sometimes a troublemaker in Greek and

Roman myth, I have personally found him to be an excellent patron for protection, strength, and courage.

Artemis/Diana

This powerful Moon and huntress goddess is particularly known as a protector of women and children.

Athena/Minerva

Athena is a goddess of war and wisdom who seeks to outwit her opponents when possible, but is also a formidable warrior.

Figure 20: Anubis

Anubis

This jackal-headed god of the Nile was a protector to the goddess Isis and her son, Horus. He is the guardian of the realms of the dead, and conducts souls from one realm to the next.

Bast

This cat-headed goddess of Egypt is very playful, but she also grants strength and fortitude in times of trouble.

Brid

Brid is the Celtic goddess of fire, healing, and poetry. Known as St. Bridget to some, she is a patron and protector of children. Her charms protect homes, children, and families.

Dagda

Dagda is the father god of the Celts, and the archdruid of divine wisdom and skill. He is powerful in all worlds, and is a wonderful god to have in your corner.

Danu

Danu is the primal Celtic mother goddess of the land, sea, and stars. Her primal power can be evoked for protection and guidance at any time.

Demeter/Ceres

As the Greek grain mother goddess, Demeter is a powerful patron for her devotees, but takes particular interest in children.

Frey

An earthy god of the Vanir tribe from Norse myth, Frey is particularly known as the protector of travelers, ships, and sailors.

Hathor

Another goddess of women's protection, Hathor's symbol, the sistrum, a ceremonial rattle, is used to banish evil spirits.

Hecate/Trivia

Hecate is the mother of witches in the Greek tradition, a triple goddess of the Underworld, and guardian of the crossroads. All witches can call upon Hecate's protective powers, particularly when crossing into new territory or worlds.

Heimdell

Heimdell is the guardian of the rainbow bridge, which leads to the home of the Norse gods. He is a vigilant guardian with magickal perceptions.

Hera/Juno

Hera, wife of Zeus, is the protector of the home, marriage, and family.

Hermes/Mercury

Hermes is the god of travelers, magick, and medicine. He can be evoked to aid and protect you on all journeys and during all acts of magick and healing.

Horus

Horus is the avenging son of Isis and Osiris. He is a great warrior and protector of the land of Egypt and his people. The Eye of Horus is a powerful talisman of protection for all who wear it.

Inanna/Astarte/Ishtar

Inanna is a powerful goddess of Earth and Sky who later descended to the Underworld to claim her power there as well. While in the Underworld, she got into some difficult situations with her sister, Ereskigal, so Inanna has a particular fondness for those who get in over their head in trouble.

Isis

Isis is the mother goddess of Egypt, the wife of Osiris, and the mother of Horus. She is a powerful sorceress and patron to both families and magicians.

Kali

Although she is not traditionally thought of as a goddess of protection, but one of destruction, death, or simply the cycles of nature, friends of mine have successfully called upon Kali as the great mother for her fierce and fiery protection. She is a particularly powerful presence when you are in fear of physical harm or are in the presence of spirits that seem fearsome to you. No spirit is fiercer than this Hindu goddess.

Macha

Macha is an Irish war goddess. As part of the triple goddess known as the Morgan, she is a protector of warriors and witches. Warriors would often mark their shield with the pentacle or pentagram, a symbol of the Morgan's protection. Macha is my patron and always appears to protect me when I need her.

Odin

Odin is the all-father of Norse mythology and patron of magicians, nobles, and berserkers.

Quan Yin

Quan Yin is an Eastern mother goddess of compassion, love, and healing. She pays particular attention to the prayers of mothers and children and can be called upon for their protection. Even though I am not a mother and am no longer a child, I've called upon Quan Yin and felt her presence quite powerfully.

Thor

Thor is the Norse god of the common man and woman, and as a storm and lightning god, can be called upon to protect anyone whose cause is just.

Figure 21: Quan Yin

Zeus/Jupiter

The father of the Greco-Roman gods, Zeus/Jupiter can be called upon for wisdom and protection.

Meditation to Meet a God of Protection

Take a few deep breaths and get yourself into a meditative state. In your mind's eye, imagine an ancient temple. This is a temple of sacred space and protection. Use your magickal mind and enter the sacred temple. As you walk down the corridor, you will end in a chamber of the gods of protection. There might be more than one deity waiting for you, or other protection spirits, such as angels or totems, could be found in this temple. You may already know each other, or this may be your first meeting.

Introduce yourself to this goddess or god. Start a conversation. Build a relationship with the forces of protection. Learn the lessons of the warrior, traveler, magician, or parent.

When done, thank the deity and return the way you came, knowing you have a powerful contact to aid you both in your physical and mystical adventures.

Cloak of the Goddess

In times of trouble, ask a protective goddess to protect you. I feel the presence of the Goddess behind me, covering me with her energy like a cloak. The cloak cocoons me in a field of protection. Sometimes I feel that I disappear in it, becoming invisible to forces that would harm me. Other times, the cloak neutralizes harm through the power of the Goddess. Simply ask to experience the cloak of the Goddess.

Mantle of the God

Like the cloak of the Goddess, you can request to feel the mantle of the God. The effects are very similar and are not necessarily based on the gender of the deity. This is how the gods I work with explained it to me: The mantle gives you a greater sense of power. It's not a typical invocation of the divine into your consciousness, but it's like wearing the mantle, the image of the godform, on the outside of your aura, giving you a sense of presence and commanding authority. This is a powerful technique, but be sure that it doesn't give you a false sense of invulnerability.

GUARDIAN NATURE SPIRITS

Various locations, like special tree groves, meadows, mountains, and other sacred sites, have guardian spirits. To enter such a sacred space and fully experience it, one ideally must ask and receive permission from the guardian spirits. When you have permission, the way is infinitely more manageable, and your work moves with ease and grace. When you don't, it seems like the resources of the wild are working in a concerted effort against you.

Many people report entering a magickal wood and feeling like they are being watched, or that some presence is with them and is not friendly. I can understand why. It's like barging into someone's home and then being surprised that they are not glad to see you.

Places of power often attract spirits of power. Some come naturally, while others are called by those who gather there, to watch over the power spot. Witches, shamans, and other practitioners routinely call for spirits to protect places of power. Sometimes the spirits are complex thoughtforms, energetic constructs with specific programs. Other times, they are spirits found in nature, both former human and nonhuman spirits, and sometimes they are what others might call nature spirits, elementals, and devas. These beings guard and guide the power site, and try to prevent those without the proper intention from entering the space. When you walk there without permission, the brush seems to hide the trail. Insects and animals may harass you. Noises distract you.

My friend Chris told me of a time in his youth when he and some friends sought out an old shaman's abandoned cave in the mountains near his home, as it had been reported that the shaman had left a gazing crystal in it. The knew they were not supposed to be there. The friends got separated. When Chris and his remaining companion found a trail, a great stag came out of nowhere and blocked their passage. They got the message that this sacred site was protected, and left.

When you do have permission, things seem to go smoother. The trail is easier. Insects bother you less (usually!), and even the brush seems to guide your way. Those who use a sacred site responsibly know to ask permission first, and to really listen for the answer. The spirits of nature do want to work with us, but they do not want to be taken for granted.

Sacred sites, such as the Egyptian pyramids and Stonehenge, are found all over the world. Every place is sacred, but certain locations host a convergence of powerful energies. I've found many powerful sites in the woods near both my home and my office. Vortexes of energy and nature spirits are just waiting to be called, assuming that you give them the common courtesy and ask the permission of all spirits and guardians present.

The process of asking permission is simple. Before entering a wood or field, to do anything, but in particular when I plan on doing magick or harvesting, I say: "Spirits of this place, I honor you. I ask your permission to enter this place. I ask for your blessing to do (name your activity, even if it is simply passing through the location). Please grant me safe passage." Then listen. If you feel, hear, or sense an answer, even if you are not sure, use it. If you get a yes, continue onward. This will open the sacred site and grant you greater access to the gifts and powers offered there.

At the end, say a thank you, such as: "Spirits of this place, I thank you for your blessing. I hope we can continue to be at peace. Blessed be."

Working with guardian spirits of sacred sites, and with all protective spirits, is quite simple. Just maintain your sense of respect for others, even if you can't see them.

BANISHING UNWANTED SPIRITS

The realms contain protective and helpful spirits, but all mythologies describe unwanted or even harmful spirits and entities as well. Usually our cleansing and clearing techniques change the energy of our environment and drive such unwanted spirits away, like shooing away flies.

At times, the spirits can be persistent and need greater encouragement to leave. Some are in need of healing and do not belong manifested in the physical world, as in the case of ghosts and hauntings. Some even try to inhabit people, not places, and also must be removed with great care.

I have found having close contact with higher spiritual forces to be the best defense in these situations. The popular technique of calling upon God for protection is very effective, but calling on any divinity with whom you feel a connection, god and/or goddess, brings powerful protection. Sometimes firm resolution and evoking the divine are all that is needed.

Having a strong connection with your own protective spirits, totems, guides, and angels will help you in these situations, giving you both protection and guidance as to how to resolve them. Each situation is different. In general, start with all your cleansing techniques. Calling upon the angelic realm through the LBRP is an excellent tool for banishing unwanted spirits.

Sound is a great clearing force. The chanting of Hebrew and angelic names in the LBRP has an inherent power to it. Some traditions of magick use toning and chanting to create sacred space. Many Sanskrit mantras are said to be protective. Traditional Christian prayers are used much like mantras in the west, for protection and healing. Singing bowls, bells, and chimes can also create sacred space. Church bells were traditionally used for both calling community to mass, and as a form of protection, for evil spirits were said to be frightened by the bells. Unfortunately for many of us, the evil spirits to the Christian church were probably the pagan gods, faeries, and ancestors, but this example does show the classic role of sound in protection and healing.

I have a friend who uses heavy rock music to clear his home of old energetic patterns. Toning "OM," the Sanskrit sound of creation, is powerful. Three OMs, usually pronounced more like "AUM," transforms the space. Each of the three sounds is symbolic of the generating, organizing, and destructive forces of creation. These are known as cardinal, fixed, and mutable energies in astrology. The Hermetic magick formula IAO uses similar symbolism for the same effect. The IAO formula stands for Isis (Nature), Apophis (the Destroyer), and Osiris (the Redeemer), the three powers embodied in Egyptian mythology. One of my favorites is a modern chant based on the five elements, to cleanse, balance, and protect a space, as well as raise energy for spell work. Here is the chant:

> El-Ka-Leem-Om-Ra.

El is for the earth element, Ka for fire, Leem for water, Om for air, and Ra for creative spirit. When done repeatedly, the vibration of a space completely changes. Try working with your own sounds and tones too.

Clearing a Haunted House

Sometimes unwanted spirits are attached to an area. They can be the spirits of the deceased that have not moved on to the next life. They are usually confused or addled. Often, they are not even full spirits, but echoes of the past. Some are angry or malevolent.

Other haunting spirits are not the dead, but spirits not at rest who were never human, possibly rogue elemental or nature spirits disconnected from their true balance.

As a public witch, I often get calls to do "de-hauntings" of homes and businesses and must say that the majority of them can be chalked up to stagnant energy, unhappy people, past traumatic events, or even bad feng shui. Only a rare few were due to unsettled spirits.

To determine if a place is haunted, first do all your own personal protection shields and rituals. Get into a light meditative state and ask to connect with your guides and protectors. As you build a relationship with them, you will be able to intuit their advice to you about a situation. You can communicate with them through the pendulum or any oracle device such as the tarot, runes, or I Ching.

If you feel guided that a space is haunted, ask permission of your guides and the guardian of the land, not the unsettled spirits, to cleanse this space. If you feel you have permission, perform the cleansing techniques, such as smudging, spraying, or visualizing clearing light. Go to every space, room, and closet to cleanse the unwanted energy.

Before doing so, I like to announce to the spirits what I am doing, to try to explain to them that they cannot remain here. I ask my guides to help the spirits who want to cross over, and often visualize a beam of white light, much like the angelic Pillar of Light, in the center of the room. Usually this will clear any unwanted spirits from the area and help them continue on their journey. Ritually, I bless a white candle for protection and light, and place it in the center of where my pillar of light will be, to use it as a beacon for spirits to move on. I might light many candles at that spot, or put a candle in each room.

Often the cleansing, particularly with incense or sage, and the pillar of light will be enough to clear a house of unwanted energies. Other times a more formal banishing is necessary. Using either my incense stick, athame, or hand, I draw banishing pentagrams in each of the four directions, as well as above and below. If you are comfortable with the entire LBRP, then do it. The toning of that ritual is often sufficient to remove unwanted energies. I then say this or something similar three times:

> In the name of the Divine Creator, the Goddess, God, and Great
> Spirit, with the aid of my spiritual guides and guardians, I ask
> and command all harmful, unwanted spirits to depart this
> place in peace, returning to their source. So mote it be!

I then stamp on the ground three times. Repeat the process in every room. Make sure the closet doors, cupboards, and cabinets are open, so the energy will easily penetrate all spaces in the room. In the case of stubborn spirits, repeat these rituals three times in a row. Usually this is sufficient to cleanse a space of unwanted spirits and move them to a plane of existence where they will do no harm and be free to continue their journey without harming you. In some sticky situations, you might have to guide a lost spirit to the next level. See the next section, "Releasing Attached Entities," for specific instructions on that. I then seal the space after the cleansing with a home-warding spell (see "Wards" in chapter 7).

Releasing Attached Entities

At times, an unwanted spirit doesn't simply attach to a place, but attaches to an individual. It is not a possession, but more like a piggy-back ride. For this to happen, the recipient is usually vulnerable in some way—ill, injured, intoxicated, or weak willed. Such spirits can also be attracted to those who have a strong powerful energy, as a continual source of nourishment and protection, or one who carries a power object or ritual tool. On top of that, such people have to be in a place where a spirit or entity is not at rest and looking for a "home." These spirits often feel parasitic in nature and are usually not human spirits, or if so, they have not been incarnate in a body for quite a long time.

Attached entities can cause or exacerbate illness, pain, depression, or mental illness. Some healers feel that such entities cling to spiritual bodies and can be carried with us from lifetime to lifetime, while others feel that when you shed your denser physical body upon death, you release any attached entities and start your next lifetime free of such attachments. Personally, as a healer and as one who has been freed of such entities, to me they feel like a pressure, both internal and external.

I experienced an attachment at an unsettled sacred site in New Hampshire while helping a couple with a public ritual of commitment. While there, I was wearing a turquoise necklace. I felt odd all day, but chalked it up to my imagination. That day I slipped and twisted my ankle. I don't know if I did it on my own, or if the spirit caused it. I was hurt worse than I thought. When I did a healing spell, my ankle was cured completely, but I immediately got a raging headache that traveled all over my head, neck, and shoulders. When I tried to psychically remove it, it moved to another part of my body. It was exasperating. When I went to a friend and healer, she had a vision of me in a forest, not knowing I had been at a sacred site, and saw a spirit go for my blue necklace, not knowing I was wearing it. I wore it as a bracelet when I saw her. She saw the spirit attracted to the necklace, not out of malevolence, but just out of seeking its energy. With her help, I released it.

Releasing attached entities is found in shamanic and New Age healing practices. They include forms of psychic "surgery" to remove attached thoughtforms and sickness spirits. The techniques start much like cleansing a home of unwanted entities, except this home is the energy body of a person.

Attempting this type of removal requires the practitioner to be very grounded in their own personal power and energy, and to have a strong will and a clear line of communication to their own spiritual guides and allies. If you are familiar with casting a magick circle (see chapter 7) or other methods of creating sacred space, you can perform the ritual in sacred space. I would also cleanse the room, including using the LBRP, before bringing the recipient into the room. Ideally, have them lie down comfortably. I do my healing work on a massage table, but the floor is fine, and to some, preferable. Most native traditions want you as close to the earth as possible, and will often have you face east or north. I start by lighting a white candle and then perform an evocation to the divine:

> *I call upon the Divine Creator, Goddess, God, and Great Spirit*
> *for guidance and protection in this healing. I call upon my own*
> *higher self and highest guides. I call upon the higher self of*

(name the recipient of this work) and (the recipient's) highest
healing guides. I ask that this be for the highest good, harming
none.

If you work with specific deities or guides, you can call upon them
by name. Then I follow a pattern of cleansing. I start with incense
and I smudge the person, raising their energy to a state that is inhospitable to the attached entity. I might also anoint them with salt water,
rose water, or a protection potion (see chapter 7) on the crown, brow,
back of the neck, wrists, throat, and any other pulse or chakra points I
am guided to anoint.

Use your intuition and guidance to get a sense of where the entity is attached. Your intuition can guide you to a specific place on or
near the body. Bring your attention to it. Imagine that space filling
with divine light. If you feel comfortable doing this, reach your
hands into it and imagine "grabbing" the spirit. If not, ask your
guides or deities to do this for you, and visualize them doing so if
they agree. Archangel Michael is usually willing to help with an entity release.

In the name of the Goddess, God, and Great Spirit, with the aid
of my spiritual guides and guardians, I ask and command that
this entity be removed from (name the person) completely and
immediately. I ask and command all harmful, unwanted spirits
to depart this place in peace, returning to their source, for the
highest good, harming none. So mote it be!

Visualize the entity lifting out of the aura of the person you are helping. I tell the person to exhale strongly and to push the entity out.
Imagine any remaining energy for the entity, any cords or tendrils,
breaking and dissolving away.

A technique for raising divine energy to banish unwanted spirits,
or change their vibration to a more harmonious energy, is chant and
tone. The god name used in the LBRP, Yud-Heh-Vahv-Heh, is very

powerful. Though many witches shun the Hebrew, and equate this chant YHVH with "Yahweh" or "Jehovah," modern witches have used it to great effect. Truly, it is not Yahweh the Patriarch, but to the Jewish mystic, the four letters of the unpronounceable name of god represent the primal creator, beyond gender. Two letters are said to be male, and two female. There is one letter for each of the four elements.

If past associations make this chant unusable for you, or for the person you are helping, I've also used the popular pagan chant using Goddess names—Isis, Astarte, Diana, Hecate, Demeter, Kali, Inanna —as a method of raising divine power to heal, protect, and banish. Any divine name can be used with this method.

Once you have a sense that the spirit has been dislodged, imagine a white light opening up into a gateway, to a higher level of energy, a place of healing and rest, over the body of the recipient. Ask your guides to take the spirit through this gateway. Feel the spirit pass through the gateway, and just as you opened it with intention, close it with intention. Imagine the space filled with healing light. I imagine the room in violet light, but many use blue, pink, or white. Use whatever color feels appropriate to the situation. Each session will be unique. Smudge yourself and any others present, including the recipient of this healing. Release your sacred space. Thank your guides, allies, and the divine. Have the recipient rest, relax, and in general take it easy.

Possession and Exorcism

Possession is when a spirit not only attaches to, but takes partial or full control of, an unwilling host. Possession is much rarer than any of the other forms of psychic attack that we have discussed so far. Usually, the spirit is malevolent and may or may not have been human. More often than not, people who feel they are possessed are avid horror-movie fans with active imaginations. In rare cases, the possession is genuine and requires professional help.

The traditional cure of possession is exorcism, a banishment of the spirit from the host. Although exorcism rituals are very similar to the procedure to release an attached entity described in the previous section, they are beyond the scope of this book and require a confident, secure, and mature practitioner. Many people fear possession, but in reality it is an attached entity. You can work with the attachment release ritual from the previous section, but if it does not work to your satisfaction and you feel a true banishment of the spirit is what is required, seek a spiritual healer, shaman, or witch who is qualified and experienced in such matters.

For more on protective spirits, angels, animals, and deities, as well as other types of guides, read my book *Spirit Allies: Meet Your Team from the Other Side.*

CHAPTER 7

BANISHINGS, BINDINGS, AND BOTTLES

Protection magick has many faces and comes in many forms. By creating your psychic shields, calling on spirits, and cleansing your space, you have already been doing protection magick. The last type of protection magick we will cover is spell craft. A spell is a specific act of magick used either to create a desired effect or to empower an object, such as a charm, to act as a focus for the magick.

Just like other forms of magickal creation, spells are done while in a slightly altered state. But unlike some meditation and psychic work, spells "launch" your will and intent into the universe through ritual. The ritual is the way to raise energy for your working and to symbolically speak to the universe. Many natural objects, tools, and ingredients, such as herbs and stones, are used in rituals. Each one carries its own vibration, from a metal blade to a pinch of salt. By partnering with these natural energies, with the spirit of the tool, you partner with the universe, raise the appropriate types of magickal vibrations, and create your effect. The study of magick is the study of the universe.

CASTING A MAGICK CIRCLE

The foundation of most modern witchcraft and Wicca traditions is the ritual of the magick circle. Primarily used to create a sacred space and contain the energy for spell work until it is released to the universe, in medieval times circles were drawn first and foremost for protection, to protect the mage from any spiritual entities he or she summoned.

The modern witches' circle, borrowing heavily from ceremonial magick, can be used as both a container and a shield of protection. It creates a bubble of energy between the worlds, a temple of sacred space, blocking out all unwanted energies.

The circle is immensely powerful, yet is not a practical protection shield. It is immobile, grounded where you cast it. You cannot enter freely in and out of the field. If you carelessly walk through it, you can break its boundaries and create a hole or burst it completely. Special procedures are used to get in and out of it. Ultimately, it is a temporary space used for a working and then released into the universe. Maintaining it permanently would create a drain on the caster's mental strength.

I have only used a magick circle solely for protection during all-night vigils for seeking knowledge, either outdoors or indoors, like a witch's version of the Native American vision quest. I have also used it in places where I have felt in danger, particularly from dangerous or unfriendly spirits when investigating homes of abuse or torment. For such situations, I also use the pillar of light from Archangel Michael.

The fundamentals of circle casting are very simple when stripped down from a specific tradition and presented as building blocks. If you already know how to cast a circle, feel free to use the methods and traditions you like best. For immediate protection with the circle, it is good to know a quick version of the casting, stripped down to the essentials.

First, have a tool to cast the circle, such as a wand, athame, or even your finger. The tool should be ritually cleansed and consecrated. Start in the north, and with your pointing tool, imagine a beam of light coming out of it, creating a ring of light as you move clockwise. The light can be of any color, but I usually see blue, white, or violet. Do this three times, with these or similar words:

> *"I cast this circle to protect me from all harm.*
>
> *I cast this circle to attract only the most balanced energies and block all harm.*
>
> *I cast this circle to create a temple between the worlds."*

Second, start by facing the north and invite in the elements from each direction, moving clockwise:

> *"To the north, I call upon the guardians of the element of earth. Guard and guide me. Hail and welcome.*
>
> *To the east, I call upon the guardians of the element of air. Guard and guide me. Hail and welcome.*
>
> *To the south, I call upon the guardians of the element of fire. Guard and guide me. Hail and welcome.*
>
> *To the west, I call upon the guardians of the element of water. Guard and guide me. Hail and welcome."*

Third, invite in the Goddess, God, and Great Spirit, in any forms you recognize, as well as your own spiritual guides and protective guardians, angels, and animals. If you have any other candles, incense, or tools that need to be lit, sprinkled, or scattered, such as salt, water, or oil, do so now.

Fourth, anoint your wrist and possibly your chakras with protection potions (recipes for protection potions are given later in this chapter). If you don't have a protection potion, you can anoint yourself with a mixture of sea salt and water. You can use a banishing-pentagram motion as part of the anointing process. In a traditional Wiccan circle, other religious elements would be added at this point, referring to gods and the working, but this outline is the barebones of the ritual. I will omit aspects that are specific to the various traditions. You can creatively add and extend this ritual based on your own guidance and previous experience.

The fifth step of this circle is called "the work," because here you do any spell work, meditation, or divination. The previous steps help establish the sacred space where you will do your work. If you are doing the circle for protection, now is when you take a breather and contemplate your situation.

Sixth, if you are doing spell work, you raise the cone of power to send out your intention. If you are empowering a charm or potion, this step is not always necessary and is up to your discretion. Empowering an object, also called charging, blessing, or consecrating, simply means holding it in your hands, thereby directing energy via your hands or third eye into it, with an intention. In protection magick, focus on the intention of protection in your mind when charging a charm, potion, or tool.

I often visualize the energy that would have gone into the cone of power going into the object of empowerment. If you raise the cone of power, raise your arms up and sweep the energy out the top of the circle in what is called the Goddess position. When you bring your arms down, cross them over the heart in the God position to reflect on your work. Then ground yourself as necessary.

Seventh, release the quarter, starting in the north and going around counterclockwise:

> *"To the north, I thank and release the guardians of the element of earth. Hail and farewell.*
>
> *To the west, I thank and release the guardians of the element of water. Hail and farewell.*
>
> *To the south, I thank and release the guardians of the element of fire. Hail and farewell.*
>
> *To the east, I thank and release the guardians of the element of air. Hail and farewell."*

Eighth, thank the powers and spirits who have gathered with you, and the Goddess, God, and Great Spirit.

Lastly, release the circle, starting in the north and moving counterclockwise once:

> *"I release this circle out into the universe as a sign of my magick. The circle is undone, but not broken."*

You can use this basic ritual outline for all the spells listed in this chapter. For more detailed lessons on casting a magick circle, review the lessons in my book *The Outer Temple of Witchcraft: Circles, Spells, and Rituals.*

THE RIGHT TIME

Much of witchcraft involves the coordination of ritual with the movement of the Moon, Sun, planets, and signs. The science of astrological timing goes beyond the scope of this book, but the simplest and most powerful advice I can give in regard to protection magick is to follow the Moon. Although you can do these spells anytime, the most powerful time is the time of the dark Moon. Just as the full Moon is the most powerful time to manifest, when the Moon has no light, the time is right for banishing harm and neutralizing unwanted influences. Many traditions say this is the witch's holiday and that no magick should be done on it, but that is because most witches focus on manifestation rather than protection.

Look on an astrological calendar for a time when the Moon will be in the third or fourth quarter. The end of the fourth quarter is the peak of this cycle, just before the Moon goes new, into the first quarter. At this time, I do my protection and banishing spells. If the need is dire, do your protection magick whenever you need it, but the dark Moon is the most powerful time for banishing harm.

PREVENTION MAGICK

Most spells of protection are not focused on specific situations, but hold the intention of protection through prevention. This magick puts you in the right place at the right time, avoiding harm. If you are in harm's way, protection magick absorbs, grounds, or blocks the harmful energy. Such spells can be focused on objects of power or fixed to a location, and are used in conjunction with previous psychic protection techniques, such as shielding.

HERBAL PROTECTION

In previous chapters, we discussed protective herbs and purifying incenses. Each on its own is a powerful tool, but when used in mixtures and consecrated in the magick circle, you can create powerful tools to protect yourself and also to give to others. Once you understand the basics of this magick, you can use the previous list of protective herbs from chapter 3 to make your own recipes, based on your favorite herbs.

The first form of herbal protection I learned was a protection potion. This potion is not meant to be drunk, but anointed on the wrists. With a saltwater base, it can be stored indefinitely without spoiling. The following formula is one of many variations of protection potion I've used in the past.

Protection Potion

2–4 cups spring water

2–4 tablespoons sea salt

1–2 teaspoons frankincense

1–2 teaspoons myrrh

½–1 teaspoon vervain

½–1 teaspoon mandrake

½–1 teaspoon rowan berries

1 piece onyx (You can substitute smokey quartz if onyx is
    unavailable)

Cast a magick circle with all your ingredients at hand. You can do this at the kitchen stove, or you can have some type of heated mixing bowl on a traditional altar workspace. I use a potpourri simmerer. Charge each herb and ask for its protection as you stir it in. I stir things nine times. I associate the number nine with both endless magick and protection, but the numbers four and five work well too. When you have added all the ingredients, hold your hands over the water, focusing your intention of protection into this potion:

> *"I charge this potion to protect the user from all harm, on any level, and ask that this be correct and for the highest good. So mote it be."*

Whoever is anointed with this potion will be protected. The spell lasts for three to four days. Potions work by bringing the plant spirit, the vibration of the herbs, into the aura of the user, and infusing that spirit into the user, conferring their blessings and the intention that was created when the potion was made. It will also help cleanse any objects or tools anointed with it. I use it on cars, bikes, and the doors to my house.

If you want to make a protection potion that you can drink, I suggest the following tea.

Protection Tea

1 part yarrow flowers
1 part hawthorn berries
1 part elder
1 part peppermint

Place equal parts of the dry herbs together in the magick circle as described in the recipe for the protection potion, but without the water. Store the herbs for future use in an airtight jar. When you want to make the tea, put a tablespoon of dry herb in a tea ball or strainer, and pour one cup of boiling water over it. Let it steep for five to fifteen minutes, and then drink. This tea will heal your aura, raise your vibration, and grant you protection. It is a great tea for psychic and emotional protection. Taken periodically over time, the results are very healing.

Although you have already learned about protection incense in chapter 4, you can deepen your knowledge by mixing your own blends of incenses. Homemade incense usually consists of resins, herbs, and oils mixed together and stored for thirty days to allow the scents to mingle before use. Then it is sprinkled on self-igniting charcoal while in ritual. Make this as you would the two previous potions, charging each ingredient in a magick circle and blessing the entire mixture.

Protection/Banishing Incense

2 parts frankincense
2 parts myrrh
1 part rosemary
1 part sandalwood

1 part lavender

1 part rose petals

1 pinch dragon's blood

Lavender essential oil (Variable; add to suit your tastes. If your
part measurement is a teaspoon, I would add 1–5 drops of
essential oil)

If you don't like the smoke of incense, you can create a protection
oil, used to consecrate people and objects just like the protection potion. Place the oil in a spray bottle with a solution of 2 ounces water
and 2 ounces alcohol, such as 80 proof or higher vodka. Mist it to
cleanse the space of unwanted vibrations and energies, just as you
would burn incense.

Spiritual Spray

2 ounces water

2 ounces vodka

5 drops frankincense essential oil

5 drops myrrh essential oil

2 drops patchouli essential oil

or

2 ounces water

2 ounces vodka

8 drops lavender essential oil

6 drops sage essential oil

1 drop rose oil (You can substitute rose geranium oil or
replace the 2 ounces of water with rose water)

If you would rather have an oil-based potion, substitute ¼ cup of a
base oil, such as jojoba, grapeseed, apricot kernel, or olive oil, for the
water and vodka. Add the essential oils to the base oil, and use it like
a water-based protection, anointing yourself, others, and ritual tools.

Protective Flower Essences

Another powerful tool to bring healing to your protection magick is the use of flower essences. Flower essences are used as a part of holistic medicine. Sometimes called flower remedies, they are usually described in the vein of homeopathy as very dilute solutions of flowers in water, preserved in a small amount of a stabilizer, such as brandy or vinegar. The solutions contain the vibration, or essence, of the plant, healing the mental, emotional, and spiritual patterns of imbalance in the body. They can be used to treat physical illness, but usually focus on the feeling and thought surrounding the illness or other unwanted patterns. Each essence has a different signature, or purpose. Some are used for grounding, and others for shock, anger, fear, or even getting along with others. And yes, a large number of flower essences are used for psychic protection.

Protective flower essences usually work by bolstering your own protective powers. Some strengthen your own warrior spirit, while others seal holes in your aura and strengthen your boundaries. Each flower has different properties. Any herb with magickal powers of protection or counter magick can theoretically be used as a protection essence. Essences bring out both the magickal and healing properties of any plant. Here are some essences I use for protection:

Angelica

Angelica resonates with the angelic realm. Its essence creates a sense of divine safety, connecting you with your angelic guardians. It also facilitates shamanic journey and spirit work.

Cactus

Due to their nature, all cacti are about protection on some level. The spikes and thorns of any plant are signatures of protection and defense.

Garlic

Garlic is an essence of protection and purification. I've used this essence for everything from psychic protection to protection from parasites, bacteria, ticks, and mosquitoes. Garlic energy is very cleansing as well.

Lady's Mantle

As a flower essence, lady's mantle provides the protective energy of the Goddess. It strongly protects our psychic, intuitive, and emotional selves.

Lavender

Lavender essence is a great mood balancer and soothes the nervous system. It also affords psychic protection and cleansing.

Monkshood

Normally a deadly poison, monkshood, in essence form, provides a feeling of safety when facing your own sense of power or working with your shadow.

Rose

Rose opens and protects the heart. It is very healing and spiritual as well as protective.

Rue

Rue grants spiritual and psychic protection. It is a powerful essence for those who fear unwanted spirits before meditation or ritual.

St. John's Wort

St. John's wort provides the light of spiritual protection to uplift you in times of darkness. It is particularly protective when doing dream magick.

Vinca

The five-petalled creeping flower called vinca is also known as sorcerer's violet or periwinkle. Growing close to the ground, it grants the benefits of grounding, but also awakens the psychic senses. Vinca can offer psychic protection when doing any type of magickal exploration.

Yarrow

Yarrow is by far my favorite protective essence. In essence form, it knits together holes in the auric boundary and reinforces your shielding. Yarrow has a great balance between feminine Venusian energy and warrior Martian energy.

To use the flower essence, take one to five drops as needed. If working with a long-term issue, such as boundaries, you could take one to five drops several times a day. The most common dose is three drops, three times a day. Take drops under the tongue or in a glass of water. They have very little plant material so there will be no scent or taste other than the preservative of alcohol or vinegar.

Most people buy flower essences in health-food and metaphysical stores. The best-known brand is the Bach Flower remedies, based on the work of Dr. Bach, the modern pioneer of flower-essence healing. Although I have used many wonderful brands, I prefer to make my own. They are not that difficult to make, and the process of making them puts you into a special relationship with the spirit of the plant. Sometimes I find making an essence more healing than taking it.

To create your own essence, first pick a flowering plant you wish to use. Sit and meditate with the plant. Feel its energy and ask to connect to its spirit. In this meditation, it may give you clues as to how to use it. Some clues are in the signature of the plant, or the way it looks and lives. Protective flowers often grow by the side of the road or the edges of gardens and forests, creating a boundary.

They are also strong tasting, sometimes poisonous, or have five-petalled flowers, like the pentagram. The plant may "speak" to you in your mind and give you all the information you need.

When you feel that the plant spirit has given you permission to make the essence, start on a sunny day and get a clear glass bowl of water. Some practitioners insist it must be a quartz-crystal bowl, but I don't use one. Clear, non-lead glass is fine. Fill it with pure water and place it next to the plant. Pick a few flowers and float them on the top of the water. This process is more energetic than chemical, so there is no precise ratio of flowers to water. Sometimes I only pick one flower. In theory, you don't have to pick any flowers as long as the water is near the plant so their energies can mingle.

Say a prayer/evocation for the essence to be healing and protecting. Draw any magickal symbols that feel appropriate to you, such as the pentagram, equal-armed cross, or infinity loop. Ask the plant to place its energy into the water. Let the essence sit in the light for a few hours, usually at least three hours. Strain the flowers out and store in a dark-colored bottle. Fill the bottle one-quarter full of a preservative such as brandy, vodka, or organic cider vinegar. This is now your mother essence. Label and date the bottle. Then you will need two half-ounce dark dropper bottles, which you will use to create weaker dilutions that have a stronger energetic effect. They become more potent at these levels, much like the potentiation of homeopathy. Ratios differ from different creators, but these are the formulas I use.

Place one to five drops of mother essence into the first bottle, which is filled with 75 percent pure water and 25 percent preservative, creating a stock bottle of your essence. This is the level of dilution you usually buy in a store. Put one to five drops of stock bottle essence into the second half-ounce bottle, also filled with the same 75/25 percent solution, and you have a dosage bottle. The one to five drops is just a guide. Some essence practitioners use more drops, or if their dosage bottle is larger or smaller than the half-ounce bottle, they adjust the number of drops accordingly. Since it is the spiritual properties we are working with, use your intuition to find the best formula for you. From this second bottle, take a few drops orally as needed.

Several essences can be combined in the dosage bottle to create a blend of magickal powers. Add each of the drops of stock essence to the dosage bottle. To create a powerful protection formula, combine several protective essences into one dosage bottle:

Protection Essence Combination
3 drops yarrow flower essence stock level

3 drops rose flower essence stock level

5 drops vinca flower essence stock level

4 drops St. John's wort essence stock level

2 drops fluorite gem elixir stock level

½ ounce dropper bottle filled with 25 percent preservative and
   75 percent water

The gem elixir is made much the same way as the flower essence, but instead of floating the flower on the surface, let the gem soak in the water, out in the sunlight. Though you can use almost any protective stone as an elixir, I favor using fluorite with yarrow. They work well together to create a protective shield and repair any auric damage. Make sure your stone is not water-soluble, like selenite, or potentially poisonous when soaked in water, like unpolished malachite. Stones in the silicon dioxide family are usually safe.

Shake the dosage bottle and take one to five drops when you need protection, to bolster your aura. Or if you are continually in difficult situations requiring a psychic and emotional shield, take three drops of this combination three times a day. Over time, your natural shields will grow stronger and you will not need it on a daily basis.

AMULETS

You can mix your knowledge of herbs, stones, symbols, and energies to create more complex protective charms. A charm that wards off influences, such as harm, or protects, is usually called an amulet. If the charm attracts forces to you, such as love, it is usually called a talisman. Different traditions use these terms differently. For protection magick, we focus on the craft of amulets.

Amulets can be made of any group of materials. They can be simple. If you carry a protective stone with you, such as any of those from chapter 4, and empower it in a magick circle with a spell of protection, you have a simple amulet that will work for you whenever you carry it. The same can be done with a magickal piece of jewelry. Simply cleanse it and link it to a spell of protection while in the magick circle. You can carry a pinch of an herb with you for the same effect.

A friend of mine carries a bit of mandrake root in her wallet for protection, since whenever she goes out, she has her wallet. She changes the piece once a year and renews the spell in a magick circle, consecrating a new piece of mandrake. I've sprinkled vervain in the glove compartment of my car for the same purpose, since I'm always driving.

As the amulets become more complex, you can use containers. The container itself can be magickally significant, from colored bags to fancy vials and metallic capsules. The color, shape, and metal can all have magickal significance. I have a little black pouch in which I carry a variety of stones and herbs, changing the objects in it as my daily needs change.

When I need to carry something with the strongest power, I combine stone, herb, and symbol in my charm. The symbols can be drawn on a piece of paper and placed in the container, or they can be painted on the outside of the container. They can also be energetically drawn into the charm, with no physical trace. All are powerful.

Amulets are a great way to combine several magickal tools—herbs, stones, color—and make wonderful magickal gifts for friends and family who are open to using them. I made car-protection amulets for my entire family and friends one year, and they all hang on the rearview mirror.

Other amulets are found in folk magick. Rowan berries are very protective. Using a needle and thread, you can make a necklace of dried rowan berries. A similar necklace can be made of frankincense and myrrh tears, using a hot needle to melt through the resin. They can be fairly fragile to wear, so be careful.

I like doing a bit of cord magick for protection jewelry. Take three strands of yarn, choosing colors that are protective for you. I like white, red, and black, the colors of the Triple Goddess. Braid the thread in a magick circle with the intention of asking the Goddess for her protection. Knot it three times, for Maiden, Mother, and Crone. Then tie it as a bracelet, necklace, or anklet. When it falls off from natural wear and tear, you no longer need that protection. Bury or burn the remaining yarn.

Remember that witchcraft is a craft, and you can add your own creativity and personal flair to your magick. Amulet making is an opportunity for creative expression as well as protection magick. You can use this example from my book of shadows to inspire your own protection charms:

Protective Charm

1 part Solomon's seal root
1 part pine needles
1 part elder flower or berry
1 part nettles
1 part St. John's wort
1 piece black tourmaline

Mix the ingredients together and empower the charm in a magick circle. Put it in a black bag and carry it with you for protection.

Travel Protection

Do this spell when you or a loved one is traveling. You will need:

> 1 white candle
>
> 1 smoky quartz crystal
>
> 1 pin
>
> Protection potion or oil

Cleanse your candle, crystal, and pin, and cast a magick circle. While in the circle, carve an equal-armed cross in a circle onto the white candle with the pin. You can heat the tip of the pin slightly in a regular altar candle to ease the carving. Just be careful not to heat the entire pin and burn yourself. Anoint the candle with protection potion. Then hold the candle in your right hand, and the crystal in your left. Hold the intention of protection while traveling. Envision your trip going smoothly and safely. Light the candle and let it burn. Place the crystal next to it. If you are performing this spell, but it is for another person, you can place a photograph of the recipient under the candle and crystal if you desire, to strengthen the connection.

The traveler should carry the crystal, and the candle can be burned down. If you are not traveling, burn a little bit of the candle each day while the traveler is gone until the candle completely burns. Snuff out the candle in between. Don't blow out the candle, or you will disrupt the balance of elements in the spell, adding too much air energy. Snuffing out the candle maintains the balance of energies between lightings.

You can adapt this spell for general protection. It doesn't have to be limited to travel.

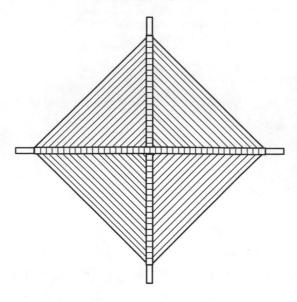

Figure 22: Witch's Eye

Witch's Eye
2 rowan or oak twigs
Red yarn

One powerful protection charm is called a Witch's Eye, or God's Eye (figure 22). It starts with a simple folk charm made by tying two rowan twigs together with red string. If there is no rowan available, oak will work nicely too. What differentiates the simple cross from the eye is the looping of the thread around each of the four ends, creating a kite-like figure. Moving clockwise around, since this is often considered a solar amulet, and starting in the center, wrap the yarn around one end and then proceed to the next. Go around the ends clockwise, moving further and further down, creating a diamond shape. When you run out of thread, tie the yard to the last end. Place the charm somewhere safe, where you want protection. I hang mine over my door, and make a new one every year near the summer solstice.

Protection for Pets, Children, and Loved Ones

One of the biggest worries is protecting our loved ones who might not necessarily be aware enough to protect themselves. It would be nice to think that the innocence of our children will be enough to save them from all harm, or that the natural instincts of our household pets will be a safeguard, but the world is a dangerous place, not just psychically, but physically. Many witches look to do general magick to protect their loves ones.

Artemis, known as Diana to the Romans, is the archer goddess of the Moon. The light of the Moon is said to be her silver shafts. Traditionally, she is known as the patron of women and children, and she is the goddess of wild things. Even as a man, I have found her help invaluable to aid and protect my loved ones.

Even though most protection magick is done close to the dark Moon, perform this spell on the waxing Moon, as the waxing crescent is associated with Artemis. It's also a great time to do this spell if the Moon is in Cancer or Sagittarius. Make some simple charm with a crescent moon on it. You can draw it on a piece of paper or wood, or paint it on a stone. Any medium for this charm is fine. Then evoke Artemis to aid you:

> *"Artemis, Moon Goddess, goddess of the hunt, please watch over (name your loved one). Protect this one from all harm. I ask this in Perfect Love and Perfect Trust. So mote it be!"*

Place the Moon charm someplace significant for you. You can put the charm in a child's jacket. I know one mother witch who did something similar, sewing a paper charm inside the jacket lining of her child's jacket so it couldn't be lost. The charm can be placed in the bedroom or, for an animal, near the food dish, buried outside, or if possible, attached to the collar. Such a charm can be renewed once a year.

WARDS

A ward is a specific protection spell centered on a location rather than a person or object. Wards are cast around a home, business, or temple to protect from all harm, from intruders to unwanted spirits. Wards can even be specific enough to block out astral travelers and remote viewers. Think of a ward as a magickal home-security system. Friendly energies, and those you personally invite into the space, can enter, but others are blocked. Although I believe in the power of wards, you must also follow up wards with real-world action. Just because you have a powerful ward, don't forget to lock your door if you feel your neighborhood is dangerous.

Home Protection Wards

Some wards are like amulets in that they consist of acts of folk magick that seem very simple, but are very powerful. Two very popular home protection spells use tree magick. The first spell uses two rowan twigs, tied in a cross with red thread, and placed over the threshold of the front door, usually on the inside. The other form is to bless many acorns. Traditionally, white oak acorns are used, but red oak is more prevalent near my home, so I use red oak acorns. Bless them for protection in a magick circle in the fall, perhaps on or near Samhain, the feast of the ancestors. Then place one acorn over each windowsill and door frame for protection. A friend of mine uses rose water on all the windows and door frames, anointing clockwise around the entire frame as she places the acorns on the them.

Another fine form of home protection is hanging an iron horseshoe over the door. Iron grounds harmful energy. Place the horseshoe with the opening down; it grounds unwanted energy into the ground before it enters the home. Iron protection doesn't have to be in the form of horseshoes. Any iron in or near your home, from an iron railing on your steps to nails and lampposts, can be magickally blessed.

A modern trick of protection magick that I learned from my friend Ardane is done when you are decorating your home. Before you paint your walls, draw protection symbols on the walls in the same color of paint that you are going to use. When you paint, you will paint over the symbols. They will be unseen, but will still magickally be present since they were painted with magick and intent.

Herbal Ward

My personal form of wards is a mixture of ritual, folk magick, and psychic shielding. First, cleanse your entire space and the space on which you wish to cast the ward. In a magick circle, take a large bowl of sea salt. In it, mix together the following:

1 tablespoon frankincense

1 tablespoon myrrh

1 tablespoon vervain

1 tablespoon yarrow

Charge the mixture for protection. While in the circle, visualize a sphere of crystal white light, like a faceted diamond, surrounding your home or whatever the "target" is for your wards. Make it the same way you made your own protection shield in chapter 5. You don't have to use a sphere, but I prefer it because I think the image of the sphere is one of the most powerful shapes. The Witch's Circle is usually visualized as a sphere of protective energy, so the sphere makes a great shape for protection magick.

Once you release the circle, take the bowl and sprinkle the contents, clockwise, at the perimeter of your property or around your home. If you live in an apartment and don't feel comfortable doing this around your building, you can sprinkle small amounts in your rooms. If there is any leftover, take the bowl and place it somewhere in the space where it will not be disturbed. I learned to place it in the basement. A variation is to place the contents into four small bowls, and put the bowls in the four corners of the basement. This causes unwanted energies to be attracted, grounded, and neutralized in the mixture. The bowls of salt must be emptied out periodically and the ritual repeated, putting new salt in the bowls. I throw the salt and powder in the ocean or bury it somewhere out in nature with a blessing.

Candle Ward

This ward involves candles. It can be done alone or in conjunction with the previous ward. If done alone, it works best for the indoor apartment dweller, since you don't have to sprinkle any messy powders in your home and it doesn't require you to have a yard. You will need the following:

- 5 black candles
- 5 white candles
- 1 green candle for the earth element
- 1 yellow candle for the air element
- 1 red candle for the fire element
- 1 blue candle for the water element
- 1 candle in your power color—your personal favorite or most magickal color—for the spirit element (Personally, I would choose violet, purple, or pink)
- Protection potion

While in a magick circle, anoint the candles with protection potion. You can carve any protection symbol you want into each, along with any elemental symbols you know.

Charge all the black candles to absorb and neutralize all harmful energy. Charge the white candles to radiate the light of protection. Charge each of the colored candles to embody the blessings of their own element. Light each candle, and then release the circle in the traditional way.

Keep the candles burning and carefully move them to each of the four "quarters" of the house, as best you can, depending on the layout of your house. If you can, keep all the candles on the same floor, even though it will protect a home with many floors. I like to put them on the bottom floor, to give protection from the bottom "up" in the spell.

Place a black, white, and the green candle in the north room of your home. Place a black, white, and the yellow candle in the east. Place a black, white, and the red candle in the south. Place a black, white, and the blue candle in the west. Lastly, keep the remaining black, white, and power-color candle in your altar space.

Let the candles burn as long as you can. Visualize their light creating a field of protection around your home. If it is late at night and you need to put them out, snuff them and re-light them later. Let them burn until they are gone.

GUARDIAN BEACON SPELL

The intention of this spell is to evoke your protective spirit into your life. You can do it before performing any of the meditations in chapter 6. It is particularly useful if you have done those meditations without great success and fear you are not connected to your spiritual guardians. Even if you don't get a direct vision or message, this spell helps strengthen your connection so you can know that your spirit allies are working to protect you on all levels. You can do it to reassure your connection when you are in stressful situations and need to feel protected.

1 candle, whatever color you feel is appropriate

Lavender incense

Choose your candle color based on your intuition. If you feel connected to a particular deity or angel, and that spirit is associated with a particular color, choose that color. If you are not sure, choose black because black draws energy to you. Start by lighting your incense. You can use commercial lavender incense, or burn the dry flowers and leaves on self-igniting charcoal. Lavender is not only an incense of protection, but it also has the power to aid in relaxation and meditation, and to enhance communication. Light your candle and say this or something similar:

"In the name of the Goddess, God, and Great Spirit, I invite my spiritual guardians into my life. Protect me from all harm, on any level. Make your presence known in my life. I ask that this be for the highest good, harming none. So mote it be!"

Let the candle burn. You can perform a meditation, or simply know their presence is in your life, guarding and guiding you.

DIRECT ACTION MAGICK

Spells of protection should not be done lightly. While most exercises in this book are a part of daily empowerment and maintenance, spells to directly influence other situations and people should be carefully contemplated. They should be done when warranted, but situations should be reasoned out and resolved on the Earth plane first. If you can solve a problem by talking to someone, try that first before resorting to specific spell work. It may be scary to talk to someone who is hostile, but call upon the fire of the spiritual, peaceful warrior. Magick comes in many forms besides banishing and bindings. Sometimes the intention of magick should simply be to peacefully resolve a situation, and then back that act of magick up with real-world action, making the gesture of peace to your enemy. Sometimes when we banish something, even with the best of intentions, if it did not have a chance to fulfill its higher purpose, then we are merely putting our life experiences on hold, to occur later on down the road, in this life or future lifetimes.

The following types of spells are direct actions, used in specific situations of difficulty. The three basic types of direct action spells are banishing, bindings, and what is classically called counter magick.

BANISHING SPELLS

Banishing spells are done to banish both unwanted energies and unwanted, unhealthy people. Banishing spells should be done with the greatest care. If someone has come into our life as a teacher, and we banish the person without understanding the reason they have come into our life, then we will attract another person who has the same purpose.

I recommend engaging in deep meditation and reflection before doing such rituals of banishment. I usually reserve such rituals only for people who are causing problems or harm, intentionally or unintentionally. Once you feel that performing such an action is in your best interests, particularly if you are ending any type of relationship and want to make a separation, you can do this ritual. Although banishing is serious, don't be afraid to banish someone from your life if you feel it is the appropriate action. Sometimes we need to take action to remove harmful forces, and banishing someone who disrupts our life can be the healthiest thing to do.

Ritual of Release

To prepare, gather some yarn, a ritual blade you can cut with, and something that symbolizes you and something that symbolizes the person you wish to separate from. It can be a piece of jewelry the person has touched, or a photo, or anything else. To release from someone with whom you have not had a personal intimate relationship, and thus do not possess such objects, you can just use a piece of paper with the person's name on it.

Cast a magick circle, and in the circle, tie together the objects that symbolize you and the other person. Call upon the Goddess, God, and Great Spirit to help you. Call upon your protective spirits. Ask to be completely and immediately released from this connection, for the highest good, harming none, with ease, grace, and gentleness. Then sever the string with your blade. Some traditions frown on using the athame to cut anything, so you could use a separate blade or even magickal scissors. I have magickal scissors, which have been consecrated, that I use to harvest herbs, so I might use those in this ritual, or the traditional boline, a white-handled witch's blade used for cutting.

When you sever the cord, separate the objects. Release the magick circle in the traditional way, and then later burn, bury, or toss into a moving body of water the object that represents the person you wish to separate from. Energetically you will be released. You will only reconnect if you focus on the person, or for some reason, consciously or unconsciously, don't want to be released.

As part of this ritual, or as a separate act, you can incorporate Cutting Psychic Cords with Archangel Michael exercise from chapter 6. Both the ritual of release and cutting psychic cords can be used to release you from ancestral or past-life energies that bind you now.

Excommunication

This spell is a variation of Catholic magick that I've heard many folk witches use. Its purpose is to completely remove someone from your life. Be forewarned: if that person is serving a higher purpose in your life, you will simply attract another person with similar attitudes and actions to fill the void.

There are many variations to the "excommunication" spell. I suggest doing it in a magick circle. You need one white taper candle. In your sacred space, name the candle after the person you wish to banish. Carve the person's name in the candle, or visualize the person's image around or in the candle. State the following:

> "I excommunicate (state the person's name) from my life, for the highest good, harming none. So mote it be."

Turn the candle upside down and snuff it with the intent of banishing. Release your sacred space and dispose of the candle, usually by burying it. Don't re-light it.

BINDING SPELLS

Binding spells are used to bind the power of a person who is directing harm against you. It's like tying their arms behind their back. They are not tied up permanently; they are only bound when they direct harm toward you or whomever your spell protects. Bindings are only done when someone is specifically causing you harm. You are binding the influence of that person in your life; you are not controlling them, curing them, manipulating them, coercing their will, or making them your friend. You are only protecting yourself.

With some binding spells, there is a healing involved, but that is a byproduct of the spell. Many protective herbs also have a high spiritual vibration, and when used in a binding, they can have the added effect of spiritualizing the situation. Usually they are used to call upon divine protection, but they can also help the person doing harm to see the bigger picture, or open this person to compassion and love. While this is wonderful when it happens, you shouldn't aim to purposely "heal" someone who hasn't asked to be healed, or to change their mind.

I knew a witch who purposely chose the lowest spiritual vibration herbs, avoiding things like frankincense and myrrh, not because of their price, but because she didn't want the person she was binding to heal or to be open to compassion. She wanted them to suffer for the harm they had created. What a horrible outlook on life! Although it is her choice, and her use of magick, I would never want someone to enter into spell work with such an attitude. I would hope all responsible witches would try to create a win-win situation for all involved.

Not all binding spells are foolproof. You need to take responsibility for yourself and your situation as well as do magick. A good friend of mine was experiencing physical pain and bleeding, which we all figured was caused by his toxic job situation. His employers were not intentionally causing harm, but were strong empathic projectors of stress, and both of them suffered from ill health themselves. After performing the bottle spell described in the next section, the situation calmed down. At times when one of the employers would normally lose his temper and yell, he didn't.

The pain and blood went away. My friend really needed to leave this job and find something that would be more fulfilling and less stressful on all levels. The job was no longer serving him. But because the symptoms disappeared, he got complacent and stopped looking for another job. The symptoms soon returned. He didn't take care of the root problem, which was to leave the job. The binding spell gave him a breather, but the true solution was to leave the toxic situation because the other people involved chose not to get better. The binding couldn't (and shouldn't) force his employers' will, but it temporarily blocked the harmful energy.

My friend's wife, on the other hand, did the same spell to bind the harm her abusive father directed toward her. He had threatened to disrupt her wedding. After the successful execution of the spell, her father simply didn't bother her much. The situation was diffused. She questioned if she could resolve and heal her relationship with her father with the binding spell in place, and thought about undoing it, but realized that the binding didn't prevent him from contacting her. He called occasionally and was pleasant, yet the phone calls didn't amount to much. He could have chosen to have a healthy relationship with her—that energy was not bound. Only his harmful energy was bound. But if she opened the bottle and undid the binding, he would be free to wreak havoc in her life again.

Bottle Spell

The first kind of binding spell I ever learned comes from the Cabot tradition of witchcraft, though there are many variations on this theme. Called the *bottle spell,* it consists of using a bottle filled with protective substances. You seal the harm directed to you in the bottle, and then it is usually placed in the refrigerator, to "cool off" or "freeze" the situation, preventing further harm. I have not done this spell often, but it always works if the cause is just. This is the variation I use. You will need the following:

1 sealable bottle or jar

Sea salt or kosher salt

Black thread

1 white candle

Paper

1 black pen

9 iron nails (You can substitute whole cloves, hawthorn spikes, or cactus needles)

1 tablespoon frankincense

1 tablespoon myrrh

1 tablespoon vervain

1 pinch dragon's blood or mandrake root

Do this spell as close to the end of the fourth quarter of the Moon as possible. Get out all your ingredients and have them on hand at your altar. Write this spell on your paper, with black ink:

> "In the name of the Goddess, God, and Great Spirit, and all my guides and guardians, I, (state your name), ask to completely and immediately neutralize and bind any harm from (state the name of the person to be bound) to me or my friends and family for the good of all, harming none. So mote it be!"

Cast the magick circle. Charge your white candle for protection. Fill your bottle three quarters full with sea salt. Bless and charge the salt for protection and neutralization. Read your spell three times, and visualize that person surrounded in a sphere of light that prevents them from directing harmful energy toward you. Roll up the spell paper and tie it with the black thread. Go around it at least three times. Place the paper in the bottle. Charge the nails and place them in the bottle. You can substitute steel nails for iron if that is all you can find. You can also use a teaspoon of iron powder or nine hawthorn spikes, nine whole cloves, or nine cactus needles, all of which are herbal forms of the protection nail.

Charge the frankincense, myrrh, vervain, and the power enhancer, either dragon's blood or mandrake, for protection and binding. Ask the spirit of each herb to help protect you. Feel the power of the bottle grow. If there is any room left in the bottle, top it off with salt. If you can't obtain these esoteric ingredients, you can substitute with other protective herbs. Solomon's seal, John the Conqueror, yarrow, garlic, black pepper, and cayenne pepper are all fine substitutes or additions. If all else fails, use a few tablespoons of protection potion if you have it available.

Close the cork or lid and seal the bottle with the white candle wax. Drip the wax counterclockwise around the bottle top to seal the unwanted energy. We go counterclockwise, or widdershins, to bind or remove power directed against us. Release the circle in the usual manner. Then place the bottle in a place where it won't be opened. Modern witches often use the back of the freezer. You can also bury it. Put it someplace out of the way. If the bottle is opened, the spell is broken and will have to be done again.

Binding Cords

Another form of binding involves cord magick. Take three pieces of yarn in colors that are protective to you. I prefer white, black, and red. Cast a magick circle. Tie the pieces of yarn at the top, and name them after your antagonist. Start braiding them together, and when you get one third of the way down, tie a knot, with the intention of knotting or blocking the harm done to you. Then, at two thirds of the way down, tie a second knot. At the end, tie the third knot, and complete it by tying the top to the bottom, creating a loop. Say:

> *"In the name of the Goddess, God, and Great Spirit, and all my*
> *guides and guardians, I, (state your name), completely and im-*

mediately bind all harm from (state the name of the person to be bound) directed toward me or my circle of life. I ask this for the good of all involved, harming none. So mote it be!"

Release the circle and bury the cord someplace away from your home.

A general protection spell can be done with a bottle or glass vial. Instead of binding a specific person, the charm is created to trap all harm and then hung in the window. Thirteen pins are cleansed, charged for protection, and placed in the bottle, along with a magnet or piece of jet and thirteen drops of protection potion or oil. Fill the rest with salt water and seal the bottle with wax. Some witches also add broken glass, nails, or hot red peppers. Charge the entire charm to draw in harmful energy, ill will, and curses and completely neutralize them. Hang the bottle in the main window of the house, and it will protect the entire household from harm. If the bottle breaks, it might serve as a warning to let you know that someone wishes you harm, and that the spell should be repeated, along with other protective measures.

Hanging a glass ball, known as a *witch's ball,* in the window is also a charm of protection. It works much like the previous Bottle Spell, but lacks any of the oil, pins, or other ingredients. The glass ball is charged for protection during a magick circle ritual. It will deflect and misdirect the energy of the evil eye and other harmful intentions directed toward you or your home. Though available commercially and in antique stores, you can find similar balls in oceanside communities as part of fishermen's nets.

For further and more traditional information on the witch's bottle and witch's ball, and many other old ways of magick, I highly suggest reading *The Witch's Craft* by Raven Grimassi.

Binding Poppets

Poppets are the European equivalent of a Voodoo doll. Poppets are used not to harm others, but as a "target" for magick that can range from healing or blessing to binding. Make a poppet, or doll, to represent the antagonist. If you can make it out of a piece of the person's own clothing, you will have a powerful tool, but you don't have to use their clothing. Don't raid their closet without permission! A lot of older books will say it must be made of their clothing, with their hair or fingernails in it. That definitely increases the link, but is not mandatory or even recommended in this day and age. Simply create a crude facsimile of the target to the best of your ability. Have black string and a needle on hand.

Cast your magick circle. While in the space, hold your doll and name it after the person you wish to bind. Thread the string through the needle and knot the end. Drive the needle through the doll's solar plexus, where the diaphragm would be. You are not doing this with the intention to harm or cause pain, but to bind the worldly power this person is directing against you. Pull the needle through, and wrap the thread around the poppet's arms three times. Drive the needle through the solar plexus again, but leave the needle in the poppet. Release the circle.

I usually bury the poppet, but some feel that you must retain the doll to retain the spell.

From the examples given so far, you might imagine that bindings only work against physical, living antagonists. They can be used on unwanted spirits and entities as well, but I do not recommend it, because to do so actually binds the spirit to the talisman you are using, such as your bottle or poppet. It's like the mythic story of the genie, or djinni, bound to the lamp. You are not freeing it to continue on its own path after it has learned its lessons. I prefer the spirit banishment techniques in the previous chapters for unwanted spirits.

Spell to Banish Gossip

After love spells, money spells, and healing spells, the next most common request I get is for a spell to stop gossip. There are many traditional spells to stop gossip, but this is one of the simplest and my favorite because anybody can do it. You will need the following:

Paper

1 black pen/marker

1 white candle and candleholder

Ideally this spell is done on the waning Moon. Take your white candle, and using a pin or the tip of a small blade, carve the Mercury symbol in it (figure 23). Mercury is the planet of communication and can be used to clear communication.

Figure 23: Mercury Symbol

On the paper, write the name of the person who is speaking ill of you in black ink. If you don't have a specific person, but a situation in mind, like if several people are gossiping, write the name of the situation, such as work, school, family, or your poetry group. Draw a circle counterclockwise around the name, and then fill in the circle. You can use a pen, a marker, or even a brush and ink or black paint. Imagine the gossip silenced. Imagine the mouths closed, or only speaking well. Let it dry and put the paper under the candleholder. Burn the candle. Like other candle magick, if you can't let it burn all the way, snuff it out and re-light it later. Once the candle burns all the way, take the paper and bury it somewhere. The gossip will stop.

To make sure the change is permanent, look closely at your own communication habits. Often people who are the most concerned about gossip are the ones doing the gossip, though they don't consciously realize it. With a change in consciousness, these situations will be transformed.

COUNTER MAGICK

Counter magick is the art of breaking specific curses and spells made by another. Sometimes they are ill wishes backed by a strong will. Other times they are acts of magick by a conscious and willing practitioner. This type of magick is also called uncrossing or hex breaking, since such cursing magick can be called crossing or hexing. They all refer to basically the same thing, but reflect different cultures and traditions.

The Old World cure for hexes is to cast your own hex. If the person who directs ill will toward you is troubled, they cannot focus their energy on making your life miserable. If you can't do the hex yourself, you hire another to do it for you. Although it varies in different traditions, usually the mage you hire to cast such a counter curse, or any curse, bears no karmic responsibility for the act. Only the one hiring the mage bears the consequences. I'm not sure I agree with that thought. Although counter curses are not an unsound magickal principle, they are not very enlightened or particularly helpful either.

Certain kinds of folk magick are designed to break the curse, like the malocchio (evil eye) diagnosis/cure from chapter 2. It is not specifically designed to return harm, but to a certain extent it does count on the fact that the curse breaker, if working for a just cause, will have the stronger will. This cure is often repeated many times and with great effort and concentration. It can make the symptoms go away, but does not always solve the overall problem.

The thought behind curse breaking is that the stronger magickal will wins, like a magickal form of arm wrestling. Whoever makes the other person go down for the count wins and breaks the curse, like breaking a rubberband. Though at times it seems like the strongest will wins, in truth such overt conflict leaves few winners, distracting a witch or mystic from the true purpose of magick and spirituality.

Counter magick can be used, but it is most effective when not waged as a battle of personal wills, but rather a ritual to unite with divine will. If you focus on your true will, the will of your highest and best self, the part of you that knows divine will and grace, you will understand the situation and find the most creative, helpful, divine solution to the problem. You will not be pitting your will against another, but aligning with divine will, not for a fight, but for a solution. You are not using divine will to crush your enemy, as some believe, but are seeking a higher view of the circumstances to resolve the problem from a more objective point of view, not a personal one. It is a hard task indeed.

Though many counter magick spells have specific rituals, depending on the type of curse placed against you, I use my own form of counter spell, guided by intuition. While in a magick circle, I have a cauldron filled with water. In the water, I pour a bit of olive oil. This mixing of the oil and water symbolizes the two forces opposing each other. I borrowed this from the Italian folk magick of my ancestors. Then I choose three counter-magick or protective herbs.

Herbs that are considered to belong specifically in the realm of hex breaking include the following:

Agrimony
Angelica
Asafoetida
Ash
Centaury
Cinquefoil
Daffodil
Fennel
Flax
Holly
Hyssop

Motherwort

Pine

Pepper

Poke

Quince

Rue

Thistle

Toadflax

Vervain

I choose and empower three herbs that I am intuitively drawn to use, and slowly sprinkle them in the oil and water. My favorite counter-magick herbs are toadflax, rue, and cinquefoil. Cinquefoil in particular is great. Called *five finger grass,* it is said that the five fingers of this leaf can undo any harm that the five fingers of another has done to you. Its spirit helps others see your point of view and, as a flower essence, helps you see other people's points of view.

I stir the cauldron with a wooden spoon or stick counterclockwise, while meditating on the problem. As I stir, I chant the names of the herbs with this spell over and over again:

Template	*Example*
(Herb 1), (Herb 2), and (Herb 3)	Toadflax, rue, and cinquefoil
By the Goddess and the God,	By the Goddess and the God,
(Herb 1), (Herb 2), and (Herb 3)	Toadflax, rue, and cinquefoil
By the north, south, east, and west	By the north, south, east, and west
(Herb 1), (Herb 2), and (Herb 3)	Toadflax, rue, and cinquefoil
Come and break this hex.	Come and break this hex.

When I feel this is done, I stop chanting and stirring. Then I add a little bit more of each herb and chant the following repeatedly:

Template	Example
(Herb 1), (Herb 2), and (Herb 3)	Toadflax, rue, and cinquefoil
By the Goddess and the God	By the Goddess and the God
(Herb 1), (Herb 2), and (Herb 3)	Toadflax, rue, and cinquefoil
By love, trust, and light.	By love, trust, and light.
(Herb 1), (Herb 2), and (Herb 3)	Toadflax, rue, and cinquefoil
Make this thing right.	Make this thing right.

Intuitively, I end the chant. Sometimes I receive a solution to the problem, an actual course of action. Other times, I just know things will be resolved, and am open to it. Release the circle, and when done, pour the water, oil, and herbs onto the ground to be released into the earth.

REVENGE, RETRIBUTION, AND CURSES

In all the old classic tales of witchcraft, you find stories of curses and revenge. Such stories are a part of our heritage whether we like it or not. In fact, some distinguish modern Wicca from old family traditions by such things as the Wiccan Rede or the Law of Three (Law of Return). They don't appear to be a part of family tradition witchcraft, or at least not an emphasized part of it. I know that in my own family practice of Catholic Italian folk magick, such ethics were not integral. The ethics were more like the Biblical "an eye for an eye, a tooth for a tooth." Curses and counter curses were part of the norm and readily accepted as the way things are.

Records of magick coming from even before the Burning Times divide magick into black and white. Civil laws governed magick before the laws of heresy outlawed all magick not sanctioned by the Church. One could visit a witch to cast a curse on an enemy. The witch was not doing black magick if the cause was justified. In primal traditions that survived persecution, such as Voodoo and Santeria, such actions are still considered part of the culture. A priest or priest-ess is not held responsible for the will of another. They are just the means of execution and are compensated for a service. Such views are cultural and I can understand them, even though they are not part of my tradition and I don't necessarily agree with them.

In modern witchcraft, opinions are somewhat split on the topic of curses and retribution magick. Though many witches feel that curses are justified in certain situations, they might not admit to it in public. Some feel the Wiccan Rede has too strong of a Judeo-Christ-ian moralistic tone. Other witches feel the Rede is the only im-mutable aspect of witchcraft, regardless of the style or tradition.

A popular saying among the more traditionalists is that a good witch needs to know how to hex in order to heal, and that is the ar-gument and danger of most psychic-defense books. If you under-stand the methods of defeating harm, the methods of causing harm are fairly obvious to you. For some, it is a standard part of training in the craft. One is not necessarily going to use the information, but it must be understood. Medical doctors, in their extensive training, learn all the ways the body can be shut down, from damaging partic-ular organs to harmful combinations of medications. The purpose of this knowledge is to enable doctors to treat their patients, not to kill them off. A healing witch could have the same type of knowl-edge and intention. I know how to prepare a cup of poisonous tea, but the same skills used to make it also allow me to brew a cup of healing tea. I choose not to use poisons, but the skill sets are the same.

The metaphysical principle behind putting a curse on someone as a form of defense is actually sound from a pure magick theory point of view. Like offering blessings to someone who is bothering you in an effort to distract their energy from bothering you, a curse will also occupy their energy, if not more so, leaving you free to go about your business. Unfortunately, if the recipient overcomes your curse and realizes it was the result of your actions, it gives them further cause to direct harmful energy to you, consciously or unconsciously, which could ultimately bind the two of you closer together

I must admit that I've known a few loving, healing, well-balanced witches who perform counter curses as a part of their protection magick. Again, I look at the intention. There is no overwhelming malice on their part. It is simply how they learned, in their traditions, to neutralize such a problem. If we compare psychic attack to a fist fight, some people will attempt to restrain and disarm the opponent, while others will just knock you out and be done with it. They accept the consequences of their actions and will not necessarily experience any major repercussions from them. Using that analogy, I can better understand their point of view. I honor them and their ways, even though it's not my way and my practice.

Some people do not focus on blessings or curses, but leave that to the universe and the gods to decide, and simply do the spell with the intention that any harm or interference be stopped. Although the result might be difficult for the recipient, I wouldn't consider that a curse, but simply a form of protection magick and defense. The Old World ethic in family traditions, and those that do not necessarily subscribe to the Rede or Law of Three, is that you attempt to work things out on the mundane level. If you don't have any luck on the personal level, you tell the person that you wish them to stop their harmful behavior, and that if they don't, you will stop them. If the behavior continues, you have given them fair warning and now must protect yourself. The act of stopping harm does not necessarily have to intentionally harm the other or be done in malice.

Coming from an eclectic background, I can see the conflicts between the different codes of ethics. I personally feel very strongly about the ethics of the Wiccan Rede and the Law of Return. In general, I feel that situations are better resolved through peace than through conflict. I believe in defense and standing up for yourself, but not in attack.

When I look at those in the craft who don't share my ethical beliefs or, more importantly, those who don't live by them, regardless of what they say in public, and who work curses maliciously, I take a close look at their lives. Without making a moral judgment, most of them don't seem happy or healthy, be it on the physical, emotional, mental, or spiritual level. It seems like no matter how justified they feel about such actions, their lives seem to reap the same results as their actions. Those who do curses seem to live a cursed life, without fulfillment or peace.

I'm most staggered by those who do feel it is morally wrong to do such things, but are willing to suffer the consequences because they want something, and so they place their personal will higher than divine will. They fulfill the worst stereotypical image of the witch.

It's easy to fall into the trap of justifiable revenge. When someone wrongs us or a loved one, when someone creates harm, particularly when done willfully and consciously, it is a natural response to want to cause harm to the perpetrator in return. When you understand how to do magick, it is easy to feel you have a duty, even a moral responsibility, to prevent harm.

Prevention is different than punishment. If you believe in the Law of Three, it is easy to feel that you are an agent of the universe, that you are fulfilling the will of the gods by personally punishing or cursing another. What goes around comes around—they deserve it. All of these are reasonable thoughts, but I feel that a witch, one who uses magick, must be impeccable in both motive and action. Witches are guardians and caretakers, but are not enforcers of universal law. The universe (the gods) is more than capable of making sure that everyone's actions are balanced and accounted for. In our limited human view, we cannot see the larger patterns or purposes. We have the right to protect ourselves and the free will to create the types of societies we desire, but it is not our job to play spiritual enforcer and "pull the trigger" of karma. Karma acts quite well on its own; we do not need to determine the way in which it will return to another.

The only retribution spell that I feel is acceptable, though I personally don't do it, is what some call "Speeding Up the Wheel of Karma." You don't do a specific act of magick for a specific result or any harm. You simply send the intention that the person who has wronged you can see the error of their ways, and understand what it is like to be on the receiving end of such behavior. Sometimes they have an unfortunate experience that teaches them the error of their ways, while other times they simply have a change of heart.

Another variation of this work is what my friend Rich refers to as "Calling the Goddess on Someone," and is used particularly when you feel a practitioner is using magick against you. Perform all necessary protection spells, and then, in meditation, evoke the Goddess. Like a friend, simply explain the situation to the Goddess and express to her that you want such actions prevented.

I feel that magick really does stem from Perfect Love and Perfect Trust. If you cannot do these actions with love and trust, if you cannot put yourself in this space, then do not do them. Magick should not stem from fear, anger, or hatred, although it can and often does. If that is the method by which you send your intentions, then that is the energy that will return to you threefold. In terms of protection magick, I keep the pentacle, with its five protection attributes, in my mind—grounding, compassion, understanding, power, and purpose—to prevent me from straying from my own code of ethics.

JUSTIFIED ANGER

Many of the dark goddesses and gods work with justified or righteous anger, and that is a powerful force, but it is not personal. It is divine. If you are motivated by personal loss rather than the breaking of sacred law, then you are not working from divine anger. You can do a spell to catch a rapist, even if the rapist has raped a loved one, and do it from justified anger. It doesn't mean personal anger doesn't exist in the situation. It obviously does, or you wouldn't be human, but you are not doing the magick for the rapist's personal destruction. You are doing magick for justice to be done. There is a difference, and although it is perhaps subtle, it can be felt.

Here, we get into the interpretation of the Law of Three and the Wiccan Rede, and try to better understand their role in our life and practice. Many of the newest generation of witches look to these rules as immutable truths that cannot be altered. "Harm none" is taken very seriously, as it should, but can it ever be absolute? In our example, the spell to capture the rapist might be forbidden. If they are performing their will and you do a spell for them to be caught, then you are harming them. You are impeding their will and controlling them. You can never do magick on someone else without their permission, and the rapist has not given permission. This person doesn't want to be caught. If put in jail, the rapist could be harmed by other prisoners. Witches holding the strictest interpretation of "harm none" believe in allowing the universe to take action rather than the witch. But if we ran our society in such a way, would any of us be safe?

Karma is a self-regulating, self-adjusting universal mechanism, but it does not always work quickly. In my own safety, I take personal responsibility. If I am lucky enough to see harm coming my way, I duck or dodge it. I don't assume that karma will take care of it before it reaches me. I would like to think that my karma or spiritual development gave me the insight to see the warning signs, but I must accept and act upon it, and put my magickal will into action, to reap the benefits. Witches often don't believe in destiny, but in magickal will, a merger of your actions with divinity.

Harm comes in a variety of degrees. Many witches think of the Wiccan Rede as a symbolic guide. The Law of Three, in my opinion, is symbolic. If something returns to you and it is a spiritual energy, how do you measure it as being threefold? I think of it as meaning that it returns to you stronger then when it was sent, stronger than double, manifesting as a reality. Good or ill fortune returning can feel tenfold or a hundredfold, depending on the situation. It is not quantifiable. It simply makes you think about your actions and their consequences. Symbolic interpretation of the Rede also prompts us to take responsibility for our own actions. We harm things all the time, but have to determine the level of acceptable harm in our life. What consequences are we willing to accept due to our actions?

We harm our food by eating it, which is one reason why many pagans do not eat meat. Some make certain where their meat comes from and how the animal was raised, creating a different level of acceptance. Even those who are strict vegetarians or vegans harm the plant by picking it, cutting it, and digesting it. Studies have shown that plants react adversely to being harvested. The flip side is that if you have a relationship with a plant, or even an animal, and are tuned in to it on a spiritual level, it will offer itself in the cycle of life and not respond adversely. All these points are controversial and debatable, creating a range of beliefs and practices in our pagan communities and in society as a whole. We each decide what are acceptable levels of harm to commit in order to sustain our own life.

We also interfere with other people's will all the time. When we get what we want, often someone else does not. If you are afraid to impede someone else's will, you would never take any action. Even actions that do not seem competitive can thwart another's will. If you enjoy music and write a song, that song could become a hit. Regardless of your intention to write and produce a hit or not, your actions created a certain result. Another songwriter may have intended to write a hit, but for whatever reason, the song never caught on.

Your song is more popular. Your song, your will, thwarted another's will, who wanted the hit. This is an outlandish example, perhaps, but our actions interfere with others all the time. When you get a job, another person doesn't. When you take the last table at a restaurant, the parking space by the door, or the last seat on a plane, someone else misses it. If we use magick to manifest these things, we have magickally interfered with another's will, yet most craft teachers tell us to use our magick to make life smoother and create what we want. These examples seem inconsequential, and they are. They are all events of the ego, or personal will.

The rules against interfering with another's will really refer to that person's higher divine will. From the divine perspective, the person who doesn't get the hit song could be learning a valuable lesson and having a growth experience from the apparent failure. The lost job could push the individual to find a job that is more suitable. The lost table, parking space, or plane seat could lead to another, and perhaps to an encounter or experience that will serve their divine will. Synchronicity happens in odd ways, but we have to be open to it.

If we save someone from being run over by pushing them out of the way, or if we do healing—from modern medicine to magick spells—when someone is in a coma, and we have not received direct permission, a strict interpreter would say that we put our will upon another in a harmful way. But I, personally, would be grateful to have my life saved in such circumstances. From a higher perspective of divine will, no harm was done. The result was healing and helpful and continued life. Sometimes there is no time to ask direct permission or meditate upon it, and we have to make a decision and live with the consequences. That doesn't mean we do magick for others without permission all the time. We use the guidelines and follow them when we can, and realize that there are degrees of interpretation. We don't live in a black-and-white world, and must simply accept the consequences of our actions when we choose to act—magickally or mundanely.

When I meditate, I repeat the intention, almost daily, that my "words, deeds, and actions be for the highest good, harming none." I do this in view of the highest divine will, since I can't help when my actions upset people on the personal level. If I have this intention and follow my intuition and better judgment, I am perfectly able to accept the results of my actions. The more I live in harmony with my divine will, the more I can discern what I should act upon, and what I need to leave alone.

In the case of the rapist, the symbolic interpreter of the Wiccan Rede would feel justified in doing magick to stop the rapist, noting that the rapist first and foremost caused unnecessary, unwanted harm to the victim, forfeiting the right to "do what you will." The criminal must accept responsibility for his actions. From a higher-self, detached position, one could argue that the soul or spirit of the rapist would want to be caught, to learn from the next cycle of experiences. We each have a role to play in society, for the good of the overall whole. The role of the law officer is to physically apprehend the criminal. The role of the witch or mystic might be to lend intention for the safety, security, and justice of the society. That divine energy may subtly help the officer in his duties.

If something is a danger to you personally or to your community, then you have a right to defend yourself. Again, intention is the important part. Protection through neutralizing a threat, in this case a criminal, is very different than hatred and malice seeking to obliterate the individual. On a magickal level, I want balance, justice, and safety. On a personal level, I might be repulsed or angry, but I do not necessarily use those feelings to fuel my magick. In the boundary of the circle, I learn to separate and connect with my magickal divine will, not necessarily my ego. The ego might provoke the action, but having a meditation practice and magickal discipline as a regular part of my life assures that I will be in a proper mindset to perform the magick in a way that is acceptable to me.

At certain times, you could feel guided to do this magick, either through a direct message from the divine, or through some inner intuitive prompting. Your personal reaction, your justified anger, might be a clue, tapping into the justified anger of the righteous gods of protection. If Hecate, Athena, Hera, Zeus, Artemis, Diana, Horus, Osiris, Sehkmet, Maat, Kali, the Morgan, Tyr, or Odin are your patrons, then such work might be a part of your spiritual practice.

The critical question is to ask yourself when this is divine will, and when it is your ego. It is quite easy to get on a personal ego trip, thinking it is solely your job to execute divine justice through your spell craft, and lose sight of your own personal and consciousness-expanding work. If you focus on "getting them," then somehow your personal prejudices, the people you don't like or imagine have wronged you, become the focus of your "cosmic" justice and you stop handling life in a normal, grounded manner. Although I do think we are sometimes called to do magick for justice, it goes hand in hand with our own personal growth and does not occupy all of our magickal time or practice. When it is divine will, it is usually very clear, and it is detached, not personal. You are being called in no uncertain terms to put your divine will into action. You simply "know" that you have to do a spell, even if the protection is not for you personally, but for the greater good of society.

Of course, when these philosophies are applied outside of the realm of crime and into politics, civil rights, environmentalism, terrorism, land disputes, and a whole host of personal, interpersonal, and global issues, the water becomes murkier. The "rules" aren't clear. Witches don't have a list of Ten Commandments saying "thou shalt not . . ." and a host of laws. We live by the laws of our land, but our ethics are very personal and complicated. They are a part of our religion and our personal relationship with the divine. We need to determine for ourselves, with divine aid, what we find acceptable. What will I accept responsibility for? Would I want this done if I were on the other side of the equation? Am I trying to stop another's true magickal will, or am I stopping the harm that is being generated by their ego will? Is this my divine will? Each witch must ask these questions for himself or herself and act accordingly.

Historically, magick has always been a practical art used in all arenas of life, from success in hunting and agriculture to victory in legal disputes and warfare. Modern occultists tell the tale of the role that protection magick played in World War II. Both sides in the conflict supposedly had magicians and witches working toward their victory. Though some say the Axis powers officially employed occultists, the Allies received unofficial aid from their magickal communities.

While the battle raged on in the material world, the height of the magickal conflict was reached when Germany planned to invade Britain. British witches and magicians cast a spell to protect the British Isles from invasion, and at the last minute, Hitler changed his attack plans, canceling the invasion. The British witches claimed victory. This was an amazing and, in my opinion, justified use of protection magick if I've ever heard of one. Given the intentions of Hitler and the horrors he caused, you could argue that the British witches were using their magick to help fulfill divine will and bring balance back into the world by protecting Britain and aiding in their success.

For me, it always boils down to the spirit of the magick. With what intention and energy are you performing it? If you are clear and are willing to accept the repercussions of your actions, then proceed. If you are uncertain, then be cautious. If you are filled with malice and hatred, then pause. Reflect, work through it, and try to become clear about your intentions.

In the end, you are casting a spell for the result you want. You can hold the intention of safety without getting into the details of what could happen to your adversary. I simply ask for it to be for the highest good, harming none, and leave the details up to the gods. I know that as long as I hold no malice in my heart, then I will not set in motion the force of malice to return to me. Those are my ethics and my way of doing things. Think about your own.

MAKING YOUR OWN MAGICK

There are all sorts of other classic protection spells found in other spell books. Some are more superstitious and archaic, giving recipes for protection against witches, vampires, and werewolves. They all have roots in classical protection magick, but usually all that is left of them is folk superstition. Very few people think about why you would throw a pinch of salt over your shoulder, but salt is a protective substance. Each action or substance has a ritualistic reason behind it, but when you forget why you do something, it becomes empty and lacks the true power of magick.

Use the basic foundations of protection magick presented here to make your own spells. Make each act, ritual, and charm a personal act of self-empowerment. Use your will, creativity, and knowledge to make the new magick of the world.

CHAPTER 8

THE NATURE OF TRUE EVIL AND THE DIVINE

Since I started writing this book, I've been challenged. The universe seems to have conspired to teach me the lessons of protection magick firsthand. I and my family, friends, covenmates, and students have been in a variety of situations that required creative uses of magickal defense since the first words were written, forcing me to make continual revisions. Some of these situations were imaginary, and some were real. Certain ones were caused by spirits, and others by people. A rare situation involved another magickal practitioner.

Originally, this was supposed to have been a simple book, designed to pass on things that I have found useful. I soon found myself challenged to find more and more useful techniques to cover a variety of circumstances and to work with different belief systems. Each difficult situation helped me expand and refine what was helpful and what was not.

Being in these situations and using these techniques in very real and serious ways for myself and others has made me really think about the deeper issues at hand in protection magick, beyond the techniques and rituals. These experiences have made me question my feelings and thoughts about the natural world, about good and evil and the role of humanity. I've struggled with how these concepts fit into my own personal worldview and how other witches view them.

GOOD AND EVIL

Well, what about true evil? You may have noticed that I don't use that word often. I also rarely use the word *negative* and try hard to avoid the blame game. So I sometimes get asked, What about evil? Are there really evil spirits and evil people out there trying to hurt the good people?

In all things, I try to be practical. I try not to get caught up in dramas. As I progress in my work, I'm not sure I believe in evil spirits and evil people. Don't get me wrong. I am no Pollyanna. I don't wear rose-colored glasses, hide my head in the sand, and think happy thoughts. I wrote this protection magick book because we must take action and defend ourselves when harmed. I believe there are spirits and people who act in harmful, awful, and evil ways. I believe there is evil in the world. But to focus on and label a person or entity as wholly evil creates a polarity dynamic that is unhealthy for all of us. The majority of conflicts, spiritual, political, social, or religious, stem from our ability to demonize others. We enter an "us versus them" mentality, where we are totally good, so therefore our enemy must be completely evil.

Think about your concept of true, absolute evil. Where do you find it? I first found it in the Christian Devil figure, but when you understand the history behind the concept of the devil, you realize it is more of a religious and political construct than a spiritual doctrine of truth. We've just been so conditioned to believe in an ultimate source of evil, and it is reflected in all our present-day myths, in movies, television, and literature. Such themes of good versus evil were not so profoundly present in the arts of the ancient pagan people.

So where do we see absolute evil now? Someone who is evil for evil's sake? I can only find that in my comic books, in my television shows, and at the movies. I think I see it when watching the news and hearing about various dictators, military leaders, or business executives. I think I see it when I thumb through my history books and see dictators, tyrants, madmen, and killers. But when I think I have found an example of such absolute evil, I usually find someone whose own past has been crossed by violence, abuse, fear, loss, addiction, or mental illness. Their own "evil" actions are a response to their experience, either to perpetuate the cycle, or to try to prevent it from ever happening again. At one point, these people were themselves victims of evil. True, they made horrible choices in response to the tragedies in their lives. They committed evil actions, but to label them as inherently evil makes them irredeemable.

We have all experienced what we call evil, if not in this life, then in past lives. We have all been victims and we have all been victimizers. We all need to see the greater pattern and help heal the individual rifts in the tapestry of life, rather than pull out an entire string and throw it away, labeling it unworthy. If we continue that, soon all of our strings will be pulled and the tapestry of life will be threadbare.

In my spiritual truths, governed by the philosophies of witchcraft and the Hermetic principles, we are all connected by an animated living force. In Hermetic philosophy, this is called the Divine Mind. We are all thoughts in the Divine Mind. There is no separation, just the perception of separation, an illusion.

A New Age practitioner once told me that evil is only that which creates a "veil," rearranging the letters. She meant that evil is what prevents us from seeing beyond the illusion to the spiritual worlds that unite us, beyond the veils that seemingly separate this world from all others.

Others in New Age communities define evil as "an absence of light." If that means harm done through ignorance, misunderstanding, pain, and fear, then yes, there is evil. If that means a primal force of anti-life, found in an individual, group, or entity, completely malevolent and irredeemable, as part of the structure of the universe, then I would have to disagree. Although dark may be the partner to light, and death the partner to life, such things are not primal forces of anti-life. The decay of a body eventually yields life-sustaining nutrients for the land around it. A death in the physical world is a rebirth in the spiritual world. Like the Yin-Yang symbol, each opposite contains the other. They are in symbiosis, not at war. War is a creation of humanity, not nature.

In witchcraft, we don't believe in an ultimate source of evil. We have no devil. Historically, we recognize such sources of evil as constructs by dominant authoritarian structures. Evil is a manmade construct having no basis in natural patterns. A sunny day is not good or evil. If you enjoy it, it is good. If you get a sunburn, then it is bad. Likewise, a hurricane is good if you need the water, or bad if it causes destruction to your property. In the end, a sunny day or a hurricane is neither good nor evil. It is just a pattern of life and nature. Humanity interprets it as good or evil based on personal wants and perceptions. It is personal, not universal. The only universal is love, which unites all things.

THE DIVINE IN ALL NATURE

In Native American traditions, there is a saying that sums up the role of humanity, nature, and the divine quite well: "It is a foolish tree whose branches fight among itself." We are all branches not only of the human family, but of the universal family. When we put our energies into fighting each other, we forget that we are of the same tree, the same roots, and nourished by the same spiritual source. Sometimes one of the other branches forgets this, but the branch that remembers should not spend all its energy perpetuating the conflict, but rather finding creative solutions to help the other branch remember.

So in the end, I don't label an individual as pure evil, with the sole purpose of creating evil and harm. Sometimes those who do harm become our greatest teachers, usually unintentionally. Often they are going through their own experience of learning and remembering. Likewise, I don't believe anyone is completely good. I don't believe in absolute polarities. We are all a mix of all polarities, as in nature. The tree, the thunderstorm, the desert, the eagle eating the rabbit, all of these are not good or evil. They simply are. Sometimes we forget that people are a part of nature as well.

Shields, spells, and charms can only do so much. The view of separation, or creating barriers between us and harm, is helpful in the short-term. We need such boundaries to distinguish ourselves and our current responsibilities from the projections and expectations of others. In the end, we must resolve our conflicts with each other because they mirror the conflicts in ourselves. As a magickal community, but also as the human community, we must shift our paradigm from separation, and find ways to build boundaries that are not walls of isolation. We are all parts of the Divine Mind. We are all one. There is no separation. There is no other. That is just the illusion, the Maya. We are all manifestations of the divine, and when we all learn how to live from this truth, we will be the flourishing tree of not only humanity, but of all life, everywhere.

BIBLIOGRAPHY

Andrews, Ted. *Animal-Speak: The Spiritual & Magical Powers of Creatures Great and Small*. Saint Paul, MN: Llewellyn Publications, 1993.

Artimage, John. www.mahatma.co.uk. August 2002.

Belhayes, Iris, with Enid. *Spirit Guides*. San Diego, CA: ACS Publications, 1986.

Black, Jason S., and Christopher S. Hyatt, P.h.D. *Urban Voodoo: A Beginner's Guide to Afro-Caribbean Magic*. Tempe AZ: New Falcon Publications, 1995.

Bonewits, Isaac. *Real Magic*. York Beach, ME: Samuel Weiser, 1989.

Cabot, Laurie. *A Salem Witch's Herbal Magic*. Salem, MA: Celtic Crow Publishing, 1994.

———. *Witchcraft as a Science, I and II*. Class handouts and lecture notes. Salem, MA: 1993.

Cabot, Laurie, with Tom Cowan. *Power of the Witch: The Earth, the Moon and the Magical Path to Enlightenment.* New York: Dell Publishing, 1989.

Cameron, Julia. *The Artist's Way.* New York: J. P. Tarcher/Penguin Putman, Inc., 1992.

Choquette, Sonia, and Patrick Tully. *Your Psychic Pathway.* Audiocassette. Niles, IL: Nightingale Conant, 1999.

Conway, D. J. *The Ancient and Shining Ones.* Saint Paul, MN: Llewellyn Publications, 1993.

Cooper, Phillip. *Basic Magic: A Practical Guide.* York Beach, ME: Samuel Weiser, 1996.

Corrigan, Ian. *The Portal Book: Teachings and Works of Celtic Witchcraft.* Cleveland, OH: The Association of Consciousness Exploration, 1996.

Crowley, Aleister. *Magick in Theory and Practice.* New York: Dover Publications, 1976.

Cunningham, Scott. *Cunningham's Encyclopedia of Crystal, Gem & Metal Magic.* Saint Paul, MN: Llewellyn Publications, 1992.

———. *Cunningham's Encyclopedia of Magical Herbs.* Saint Paul, MN: Llewellyn Publications, 1985.

———. *Incense, Oils and Brews.* Saint Paul, MN: Llewellyn Publications, 1989.

Davidson, Gustav. *A Dictionary of Angels, Including the Fallen Angels.* New York: The Free Press, 1967.

Denning, Melita, and Osborne Phillips. *Practical Guide to Psychic Self-Defense and Well-Being.* Saint Paul, MN: Llewellyn Publications, 1987.

Farrar, Janet and Stewart. *Spells and How They Work.* Custer, WA: Phoenix Publishing, 1990.

Fortune, Dion. *Psychic Self Defense.* Boston, MA: Red Wheel/Weiser, 2001.

Grimassi, Raven. *The Witches' Craft*. Saint Paul, MN: Llewellyn Publications, 2002.

Guiley, Rosemary Ellen. *The Encyclopedia of Witches & Witchcraft*. New York: Checkmark Books, 1999.

Harner, Michael. *The Way of the Shaman*. Third edition. New York: HarperCollins, 1990.

Hine, Phil. *Condensed Chaos*. Tempe, AZ: New Falcon, 1995.

Kraig, Donald Michael. *Modern Magick: Eleven Lessons in the High Magickal Arts*. Saint Paul, MN: Llewellyn Publications, 1988.

The Kybalion: Hermetic Philosophy by Three Initiates. Chicago, IL: The Yogi Publication Society, 1912.

Penczak, Christopher. *City Magick: Urban Rituals, Spells and Shamanism*. York Beach, ME: Samuel Weiser, 2000.

———. *The Inner Temple of Witchcraft: Magick, Meditation and Psychic Development*. Saint Paul, MN: Llewellyn Publications, 2002.

———. *Spirit Allies: Meet Your Team from the Other Side*. Boston, MA: Samuel Weiser, 2001.

Peschel, Lisa. *A Practical Guide to the Runes: Their Uses in Divination and Magick*. Saint Paul, MN: Llewellyn Publications, 1989.

Sanchez, Victor. *The Teachings of Don Carlos*. Santa Fe, NM: Bear & Company, 1995.

Teish, Luisah. *Jambalaya: The Natural Woman's Book of Personal Charms and Practical Rituals*. San Francisco, CA: HarperCollins, 1988.

Thorsson, Edred. *The Book of Ogham*. Saint Paul, MN: Llewellyn Publications, 1994.

Valiente, Doreen. *An ABC of Witchcraft Past and Present*. New York: St. Martin's Press, 1973.

Yin, Amorah Quan. *The Pleiadian Workbook: Awaking Your Divine Ka*. Santa Fe, NM, Bear & Company, 1996.

INDEX

ABOUT THE AUTHOR

Christopher Penczak (New Hampshire) teaches classes throughout New England on witchcraft, meditation, Reiki, crystals, and shamanic journey. He is the author of *The Inner Temple of Witchcraft* and *The Outer Temple of Witchcraft,* and writes for several local and national metaphysical magazines.